ADVICE TO A DANCER

Wisdom and Wonder from the Studio and Stage

Written and Photographed by
Julian Adair

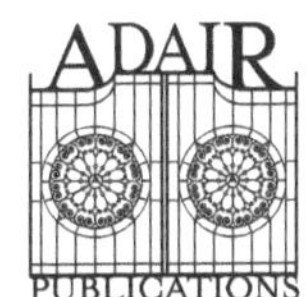

Omaha, Nebraska

Hardcover ISBN: 978-0-9988618-2-1

Paperback ISBN: 978-0-9988618-1-4

Cataloging-in-Publication data on file with the publisher.

Adair Publications

13518 L. Street,
Omaha, NE 68137

adairdance@gmail.com

AdairDance.com

Production and marketing: Concierge Marketing Inc.

Printed in the United States of America

10 9 8 7 6 5 4 3 2 1

Introduction

Advice to a Dancer was originally written during a summer writers' workshop, Fine Lines, and was published in the fall 2010 quarterly edition. When I wrote this piece, I had always hoped there would one day be a visual component. Little did I know or ever dream that it would be a composition of my own. It wasn't until March of 2012 that this element came into being, and when my photography became a prominent part of my creative life.

One of the most difficult challenges facing a choreographer and performing artist is how to meld music and movement into an artistic statement that will have an impact on an audience. Performance exists only in the present, but when it is captured by the lens of a camera, a permanent memory is created.

Being a creator of dance for most of my life and a dance educator for over three decades has given me the opportunity to create, produce and teach in numerous settings. As a choreographer and performing artist, I have always seen movement, line, color, texture and gestures in music, art and everyday surroundings, which provide great groundwork when photographing.

Creating work for the stage is extraordinary, and among my favorite classes is composition: teaching and guiding young choreographers into the world of creating art through movement. Regardless of the medium, the laws of composition are universal, and the themes written here are universal no matter your style, technique or experience. Applying this skill in composing dance can also be applied through a camera lens, creating choreography for the printed page.

These photos capture an inherent quality of creativity. The dancers bring natural talents, skill and presence to the stage and to each photography page, demonstrating how dance brings them to places only reached when one is in motion.

Any journey is a result of those who went before us, who mentored, taught, blazed trails, encouraged, imparted wisdom, shared experiences and challenges. There are many people who had a hand in furthering my journey to creating this book and so many of my creative adventures. To every teacher that I have encountered, for the training, insights and experiences. To David Martin and Fine Lines for the support, encouragement and belief in my written word. To Billy Sobczyk for his insights and creativity. To John Adair for his wisdom and inspiration. To Jim Williams, dancer, photographer, mentor and friend. To my family and the many others who danced their way across my studio or stage, thank you.

Dance on…

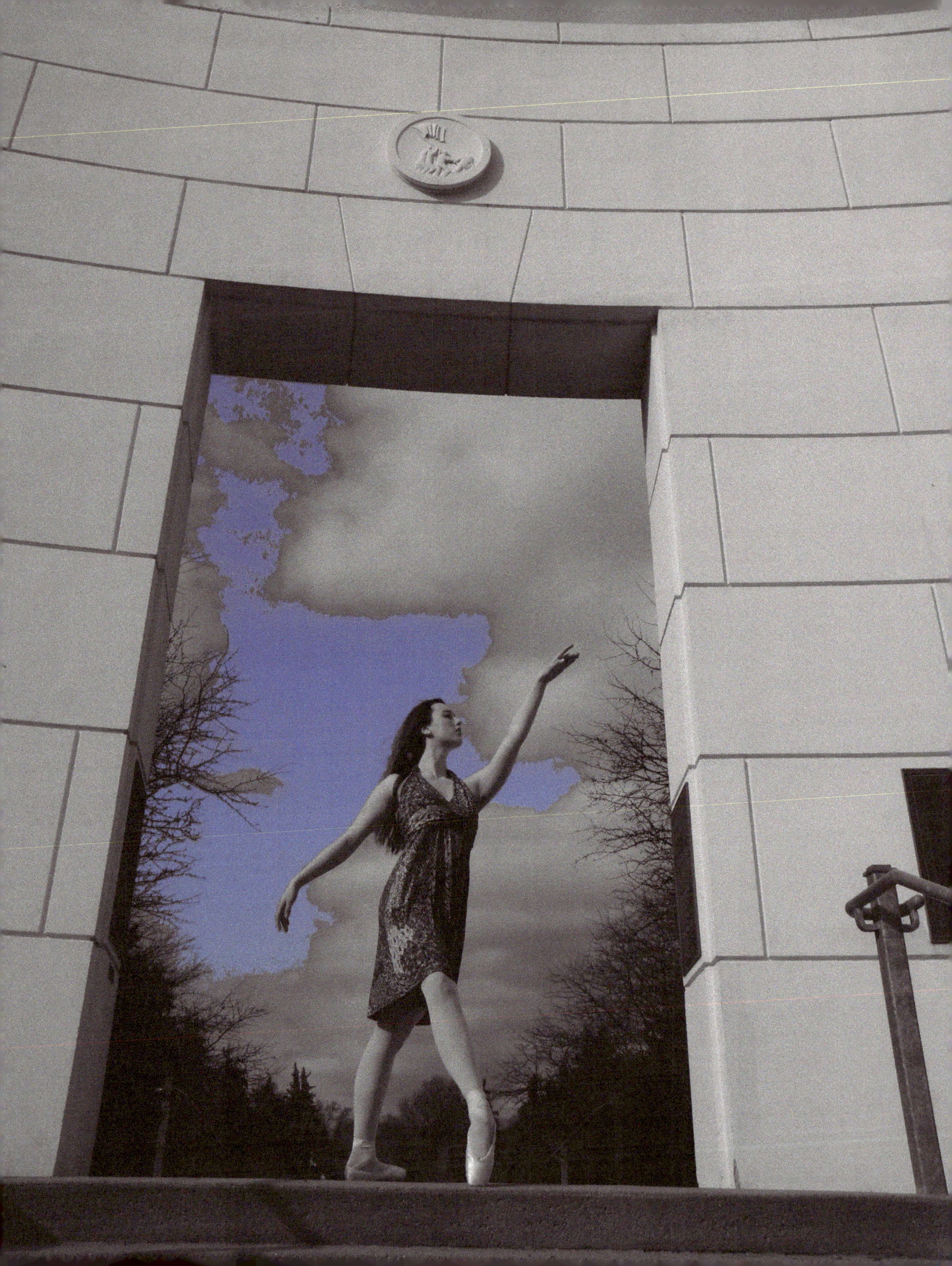

Stand tall, proud and grounded

Stretch a little further each day

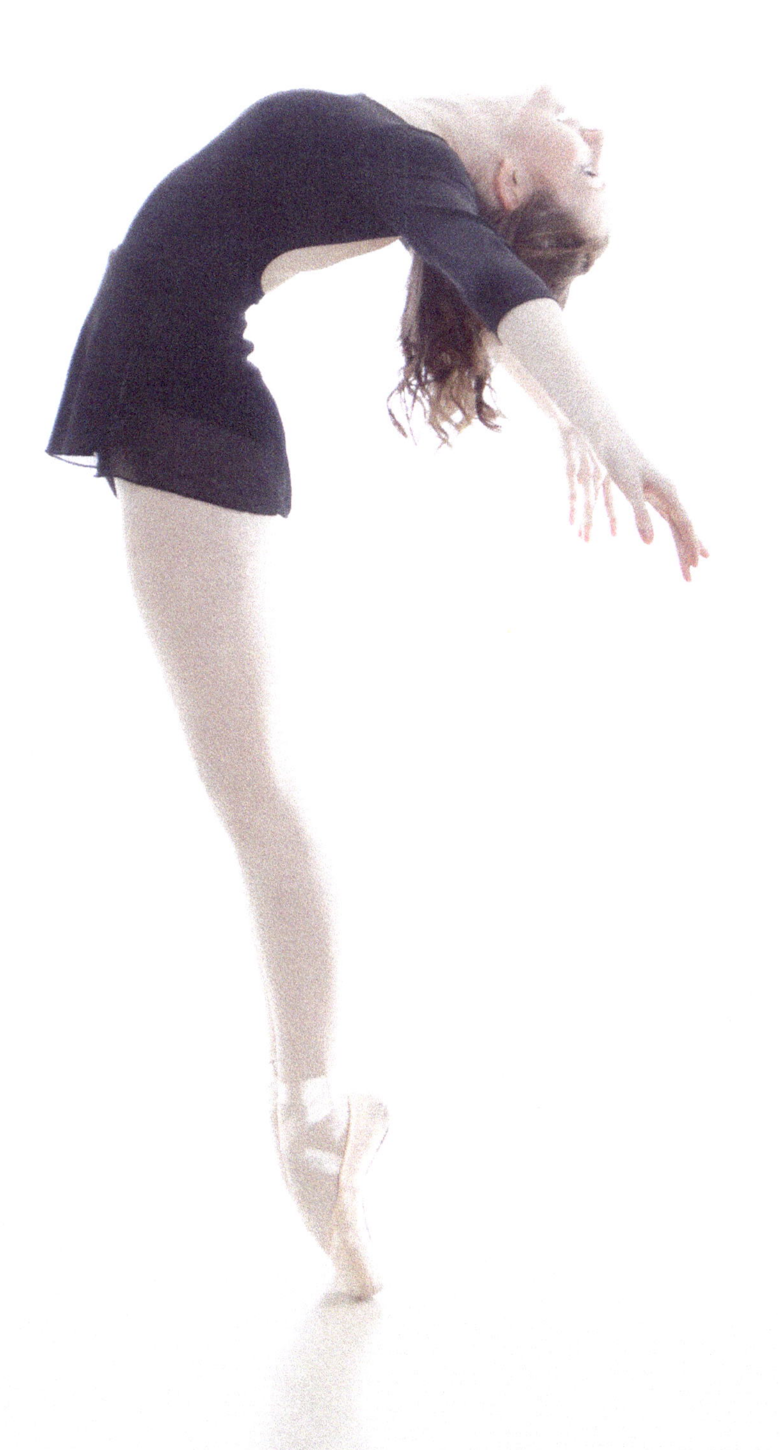

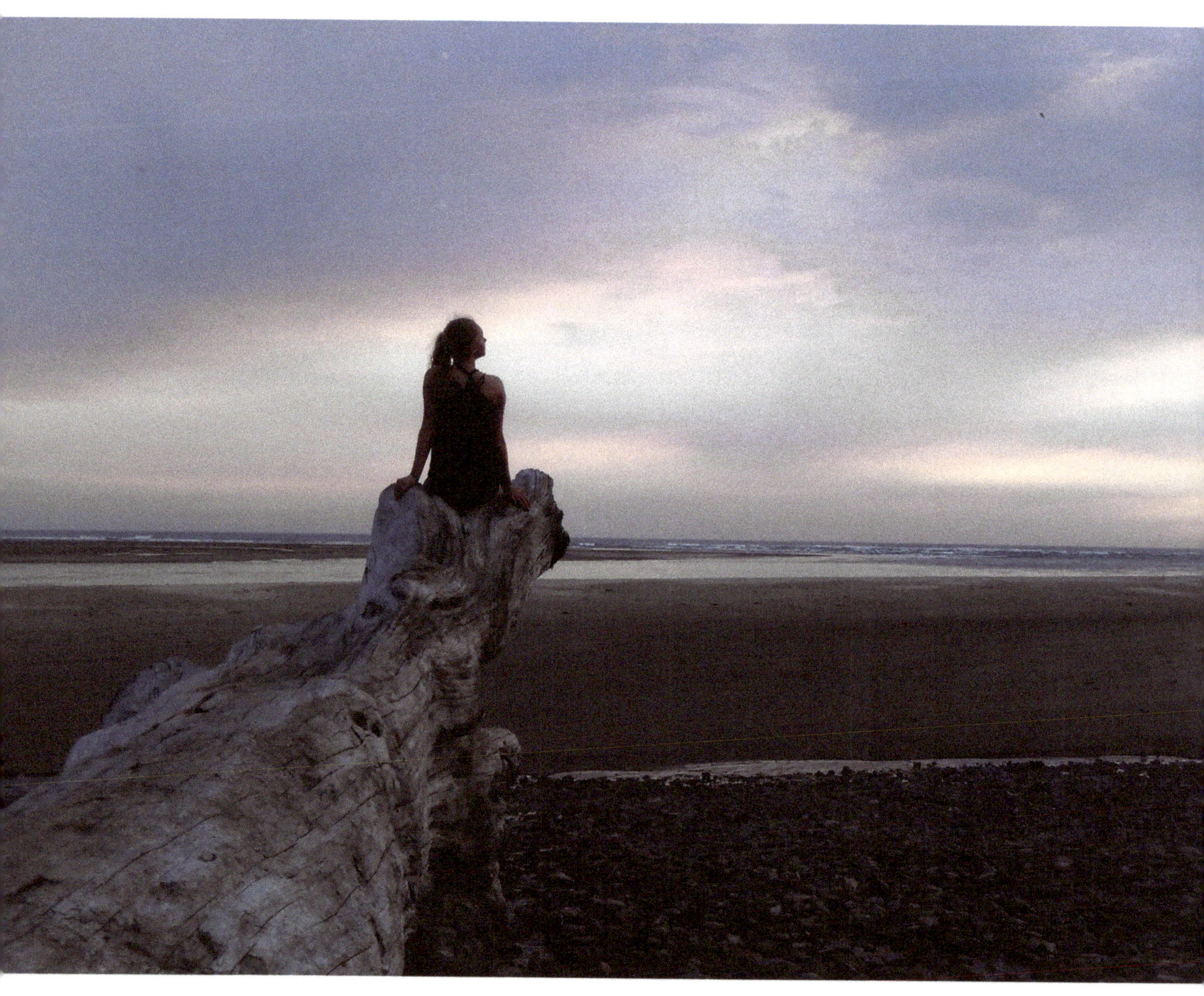

Take time to nourish
your body and mind

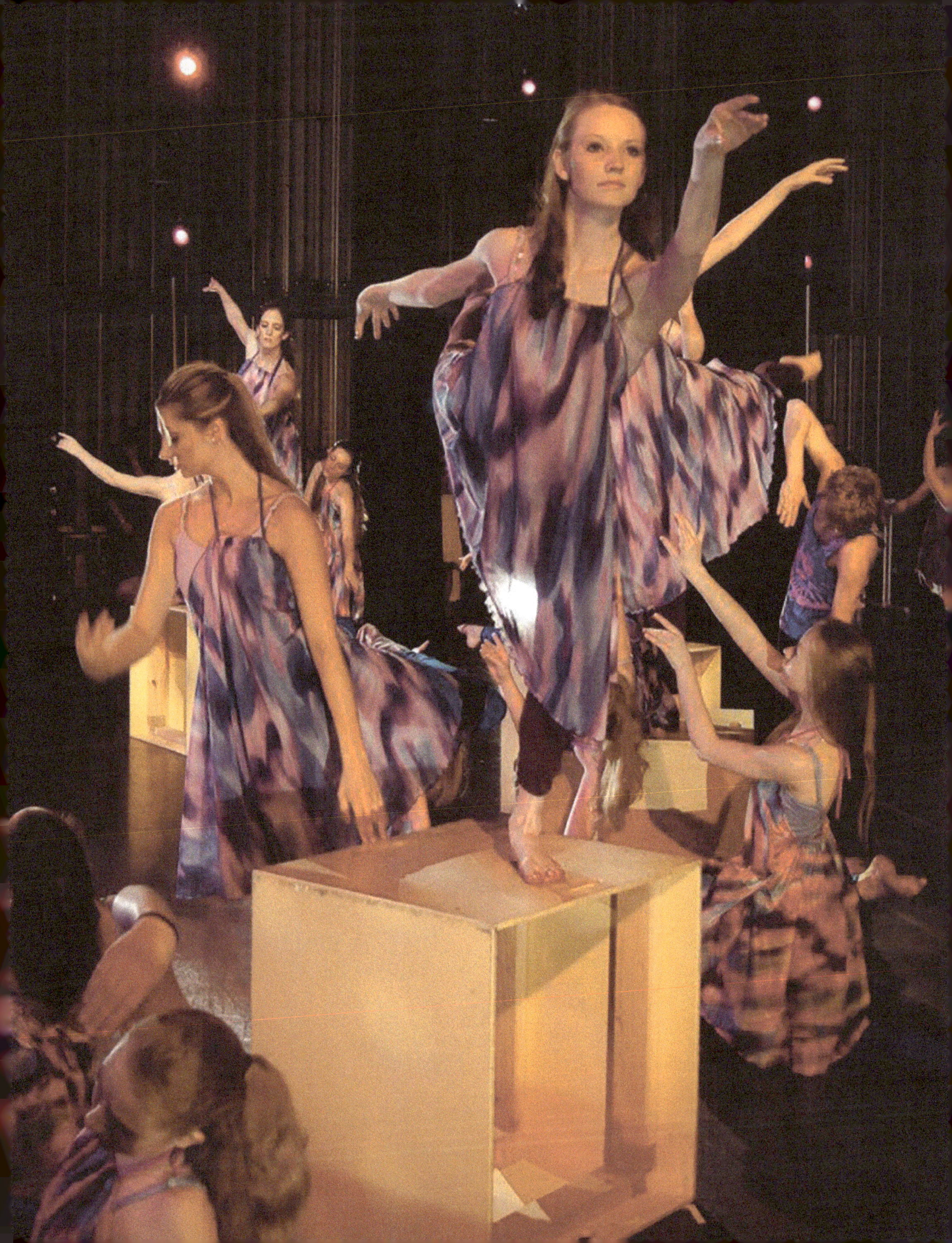

Be aware

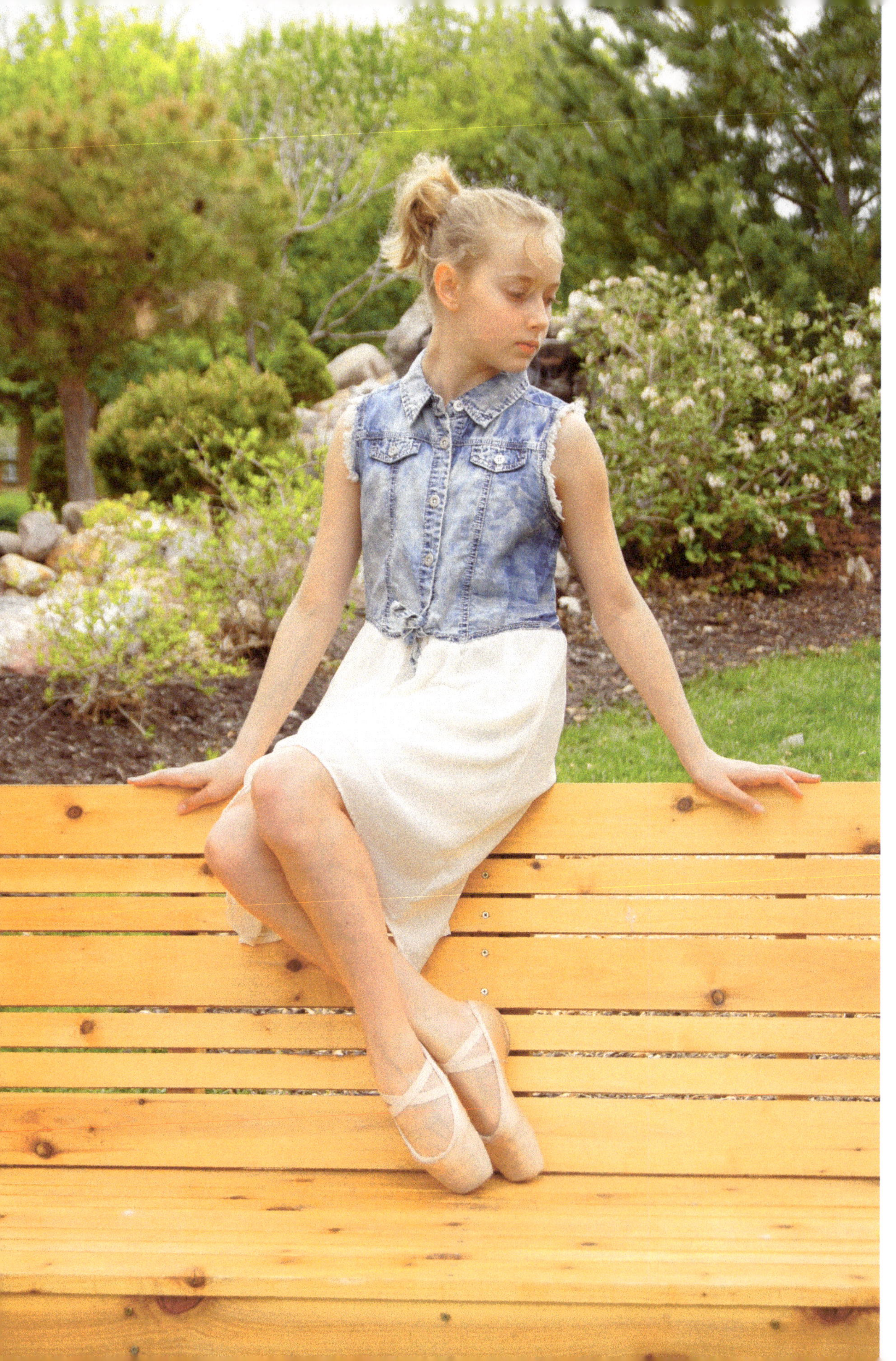

Rest, Watch

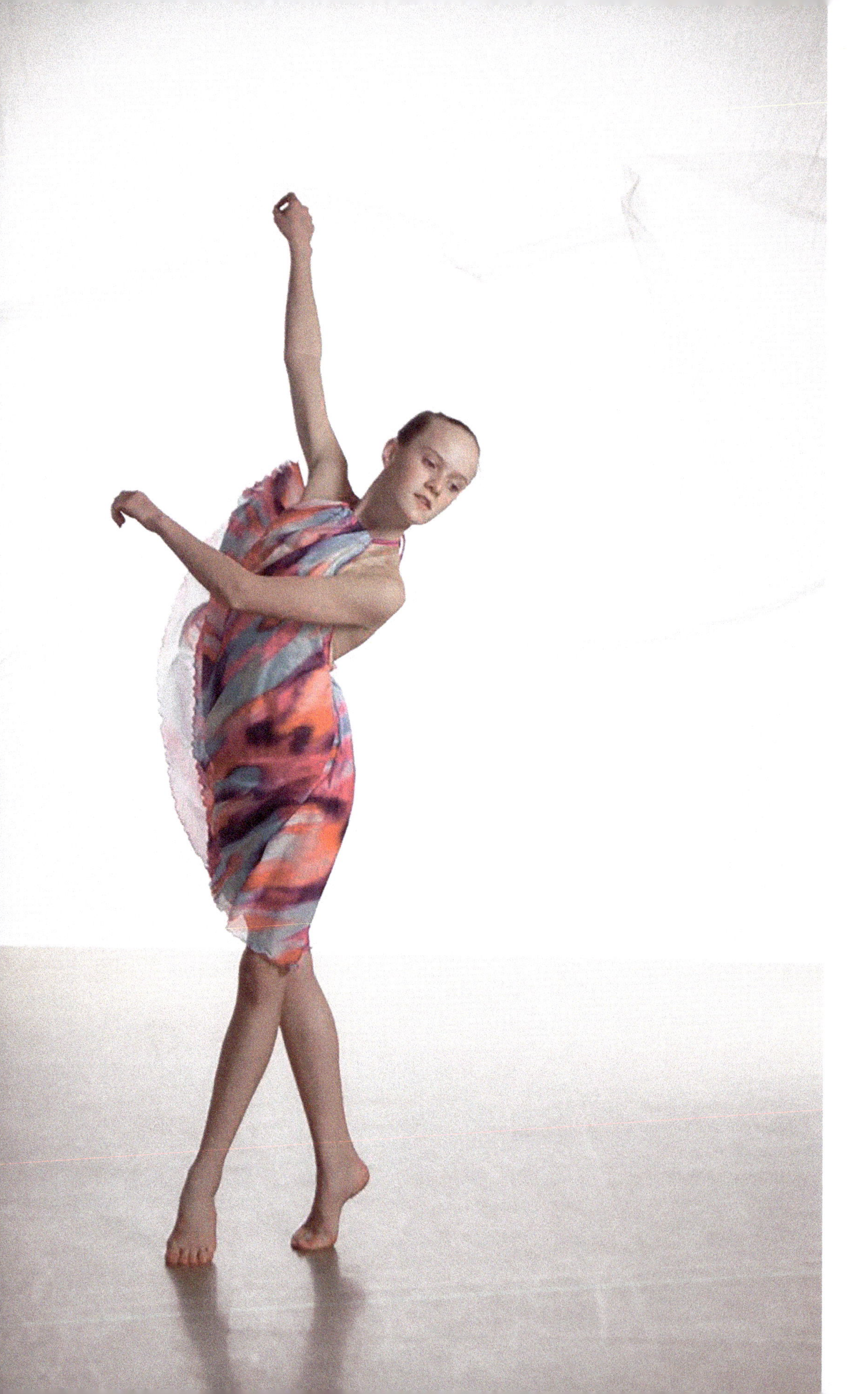

Try, Practice

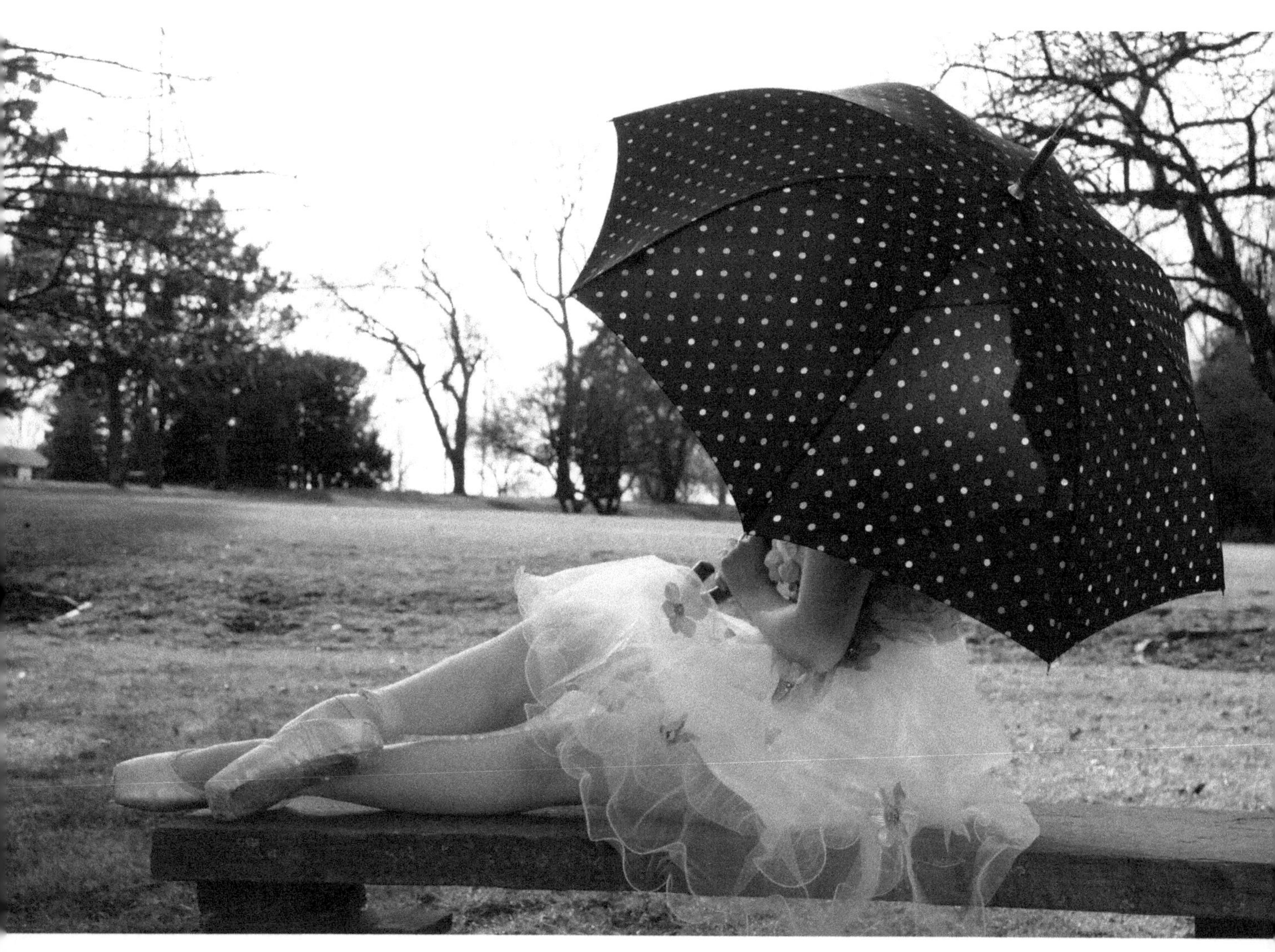

Be prepared

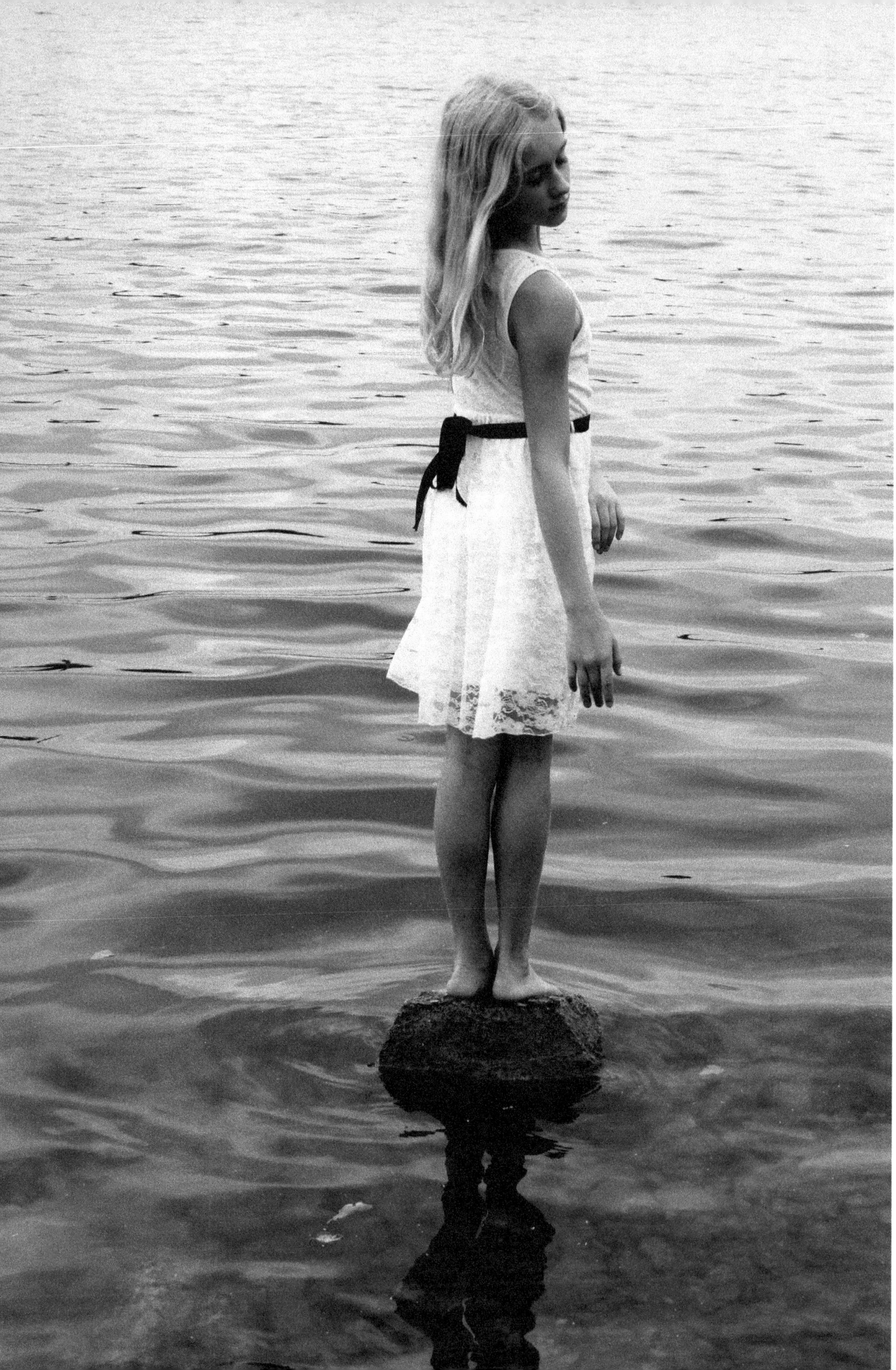

Allow yourself to make
mistakes… they are gifts

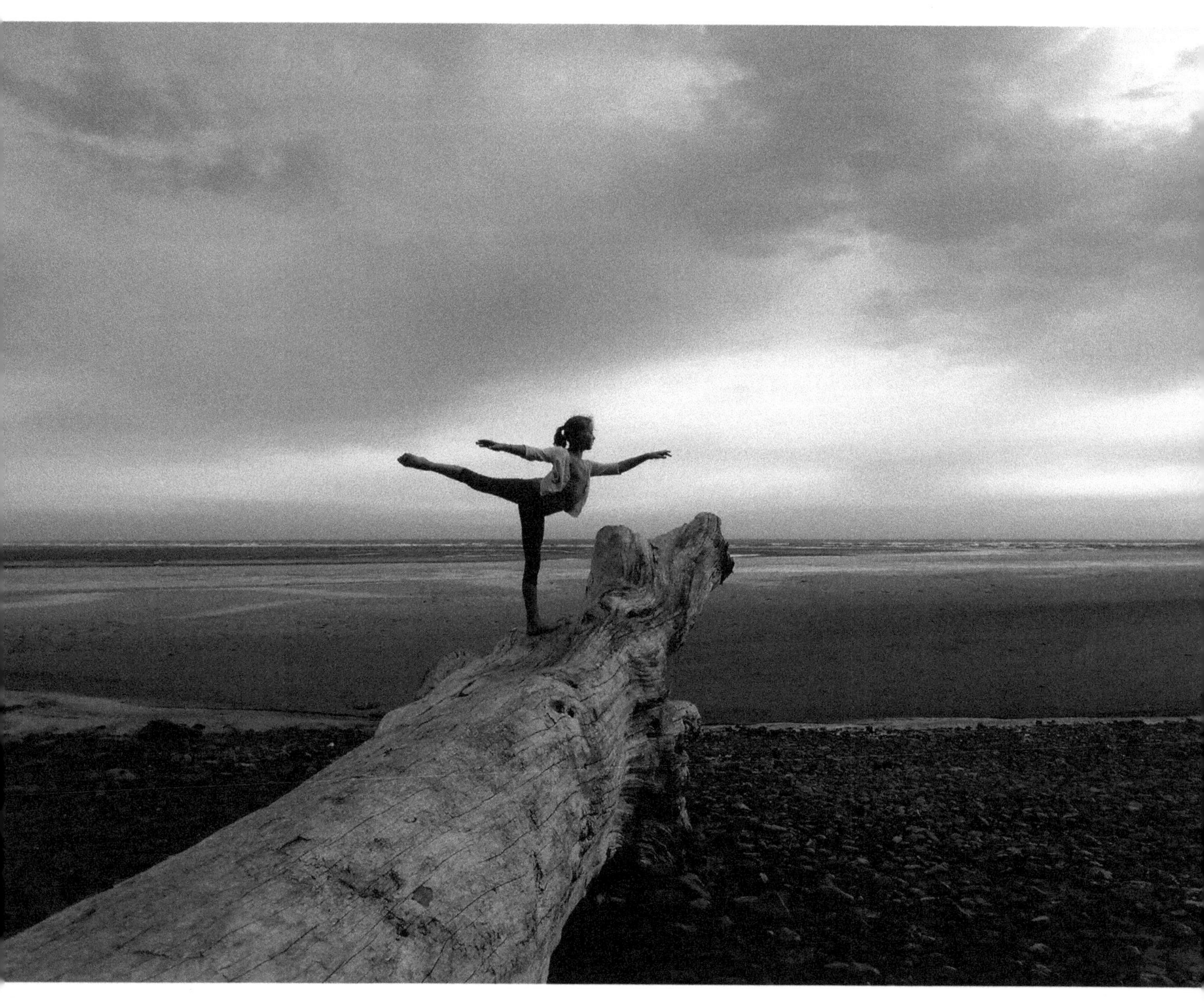

Find inspiration

Practice like you want to perform

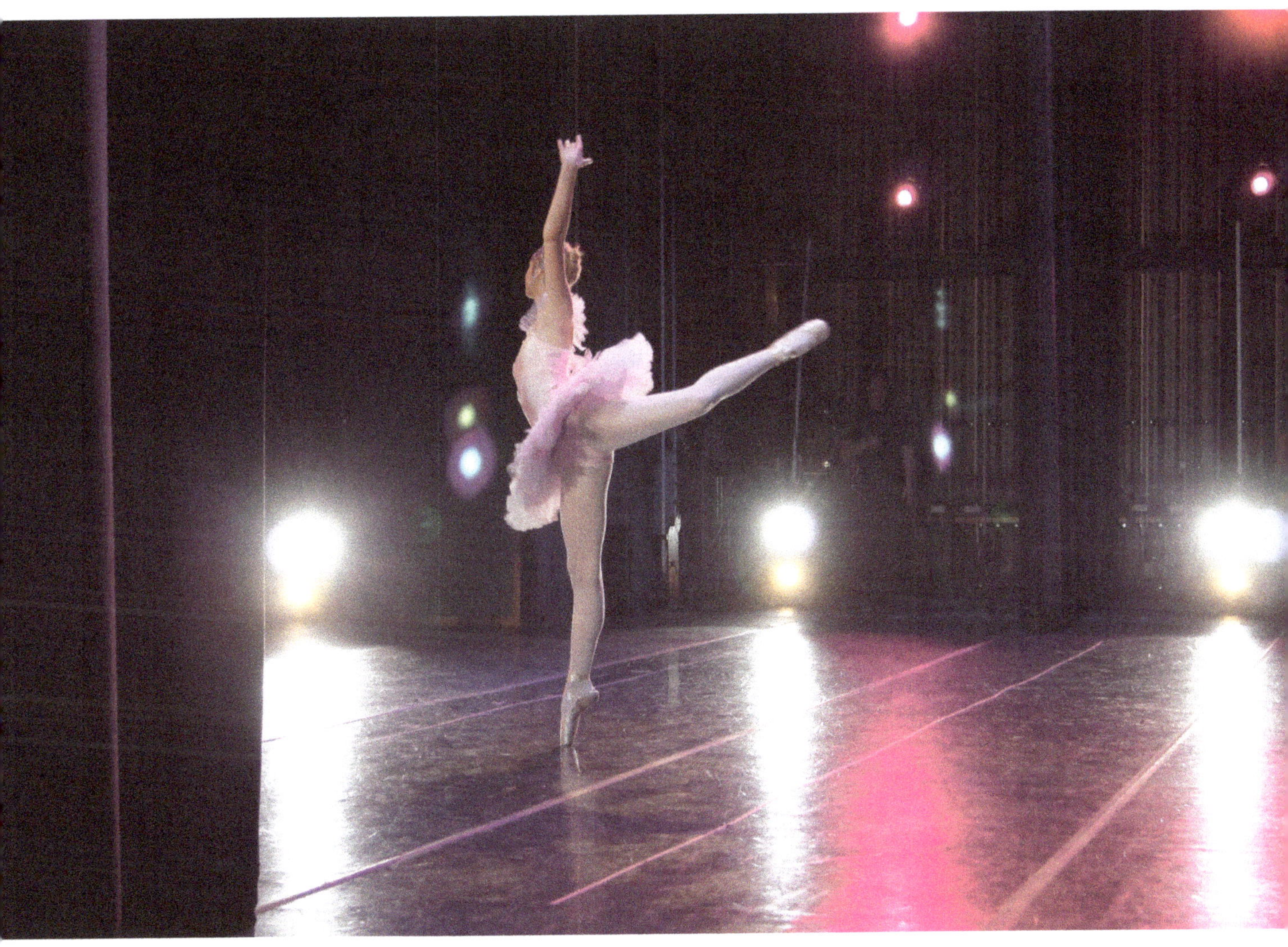

Change: it can be hard,
it can be good, it is inevitable

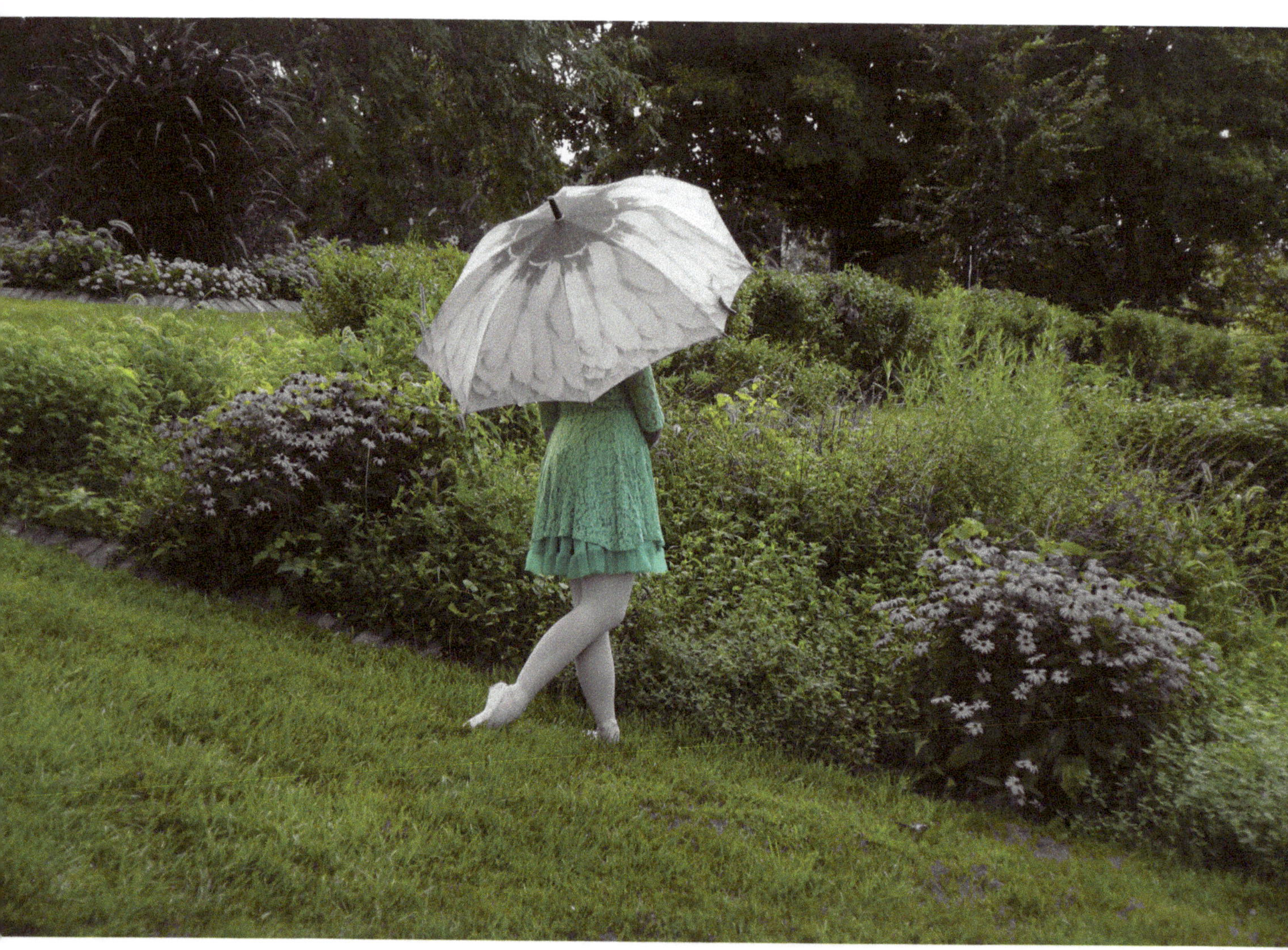

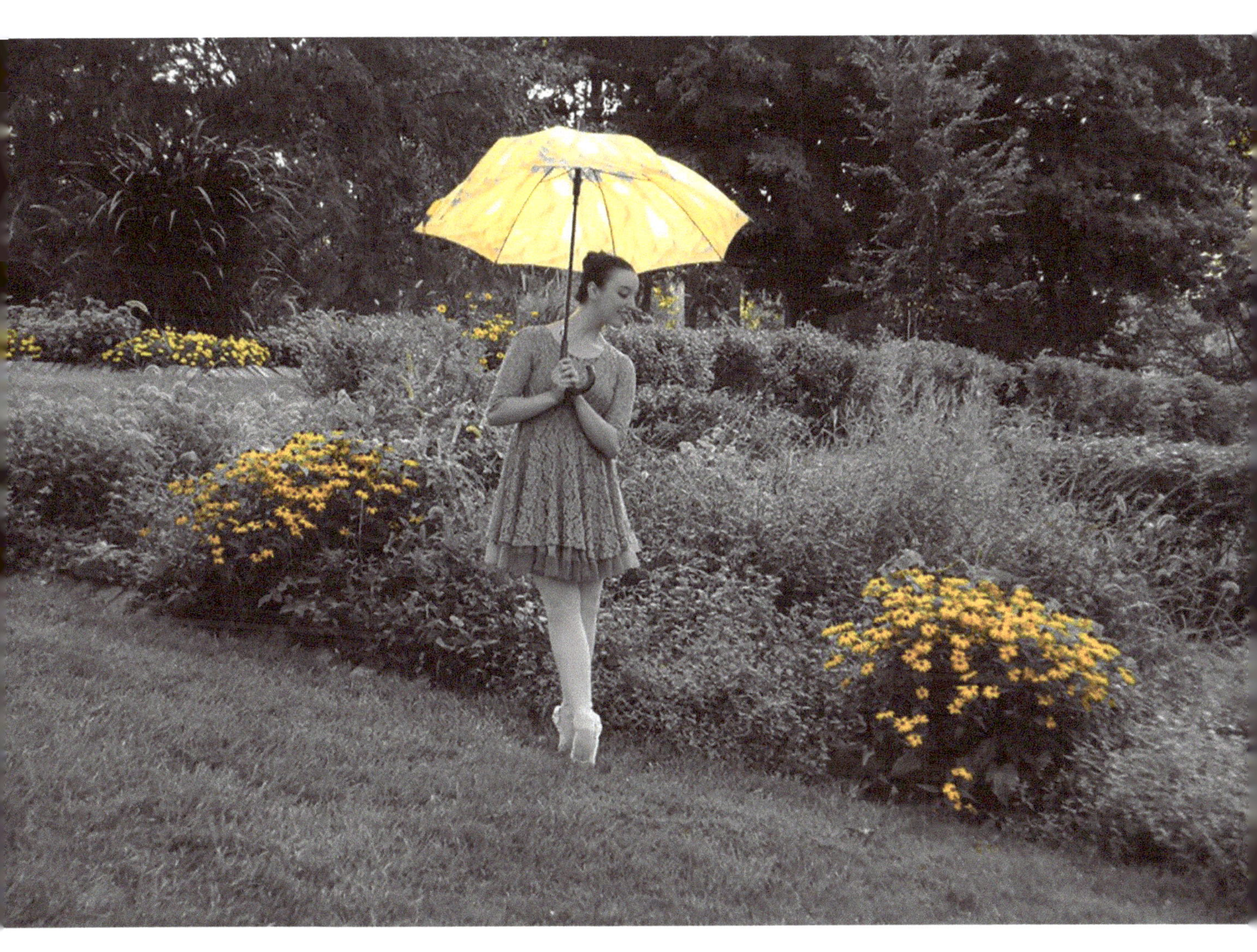

Embrace it, grow from it

Dress the part

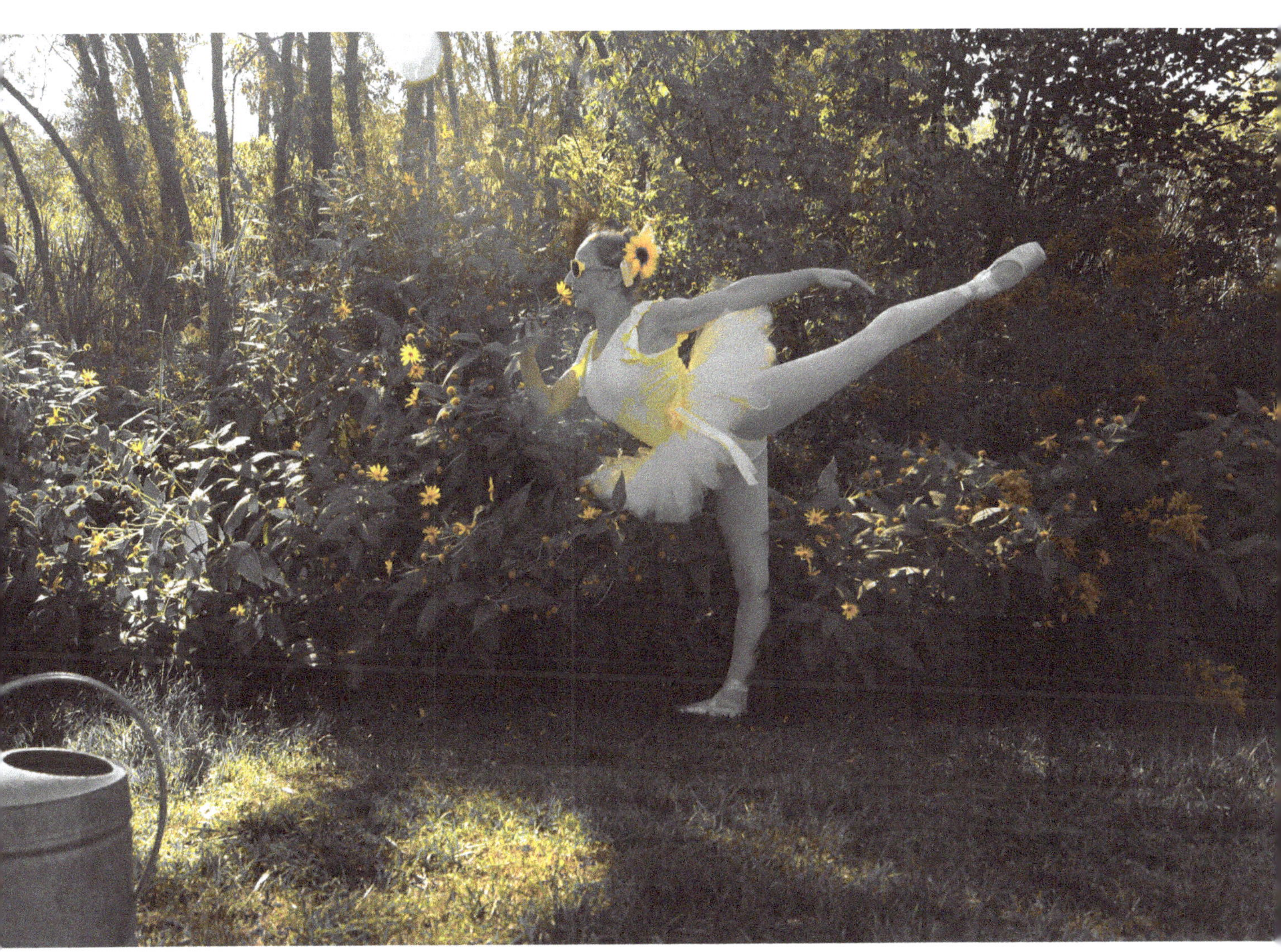

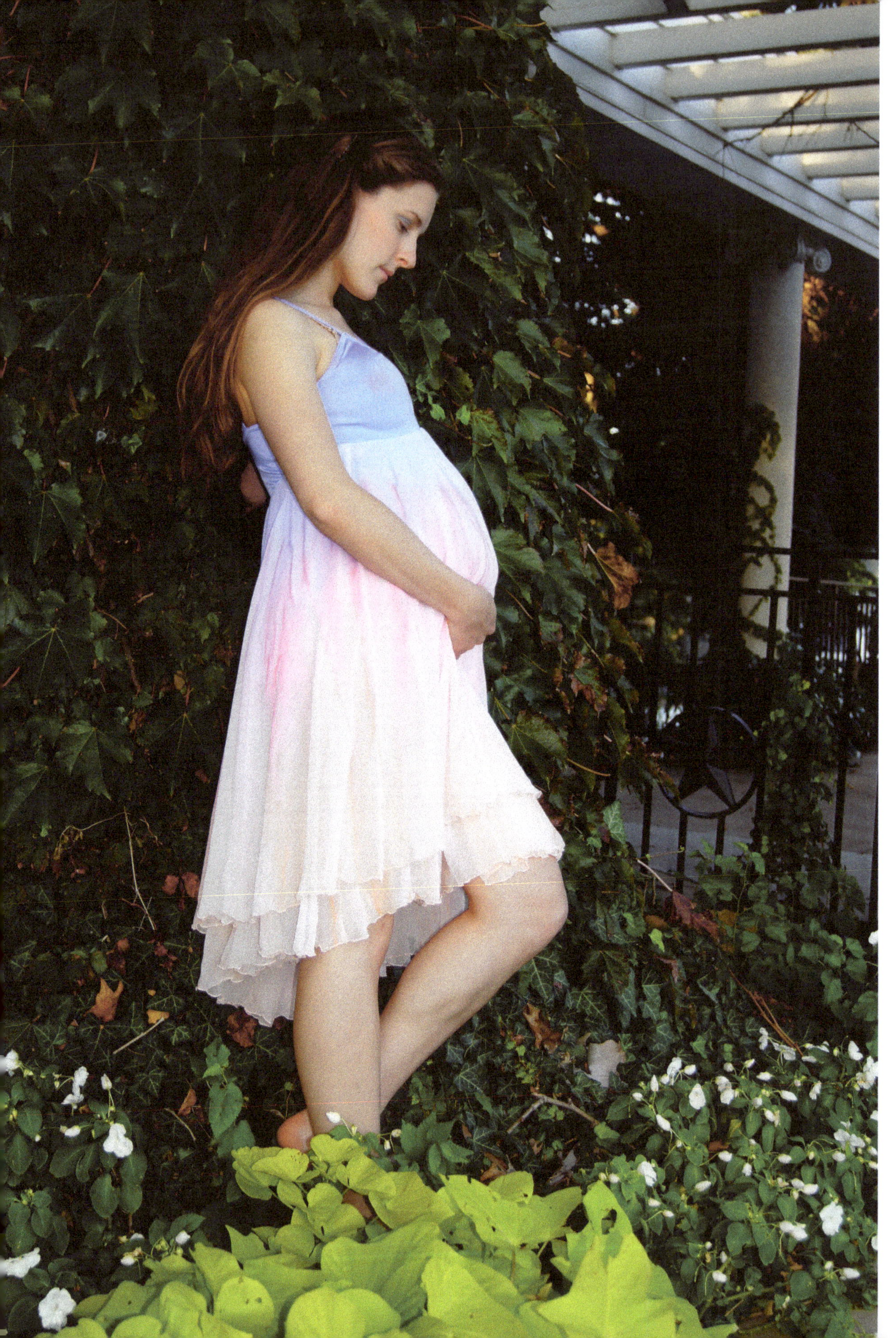

Focus and breathe,
and breathe again

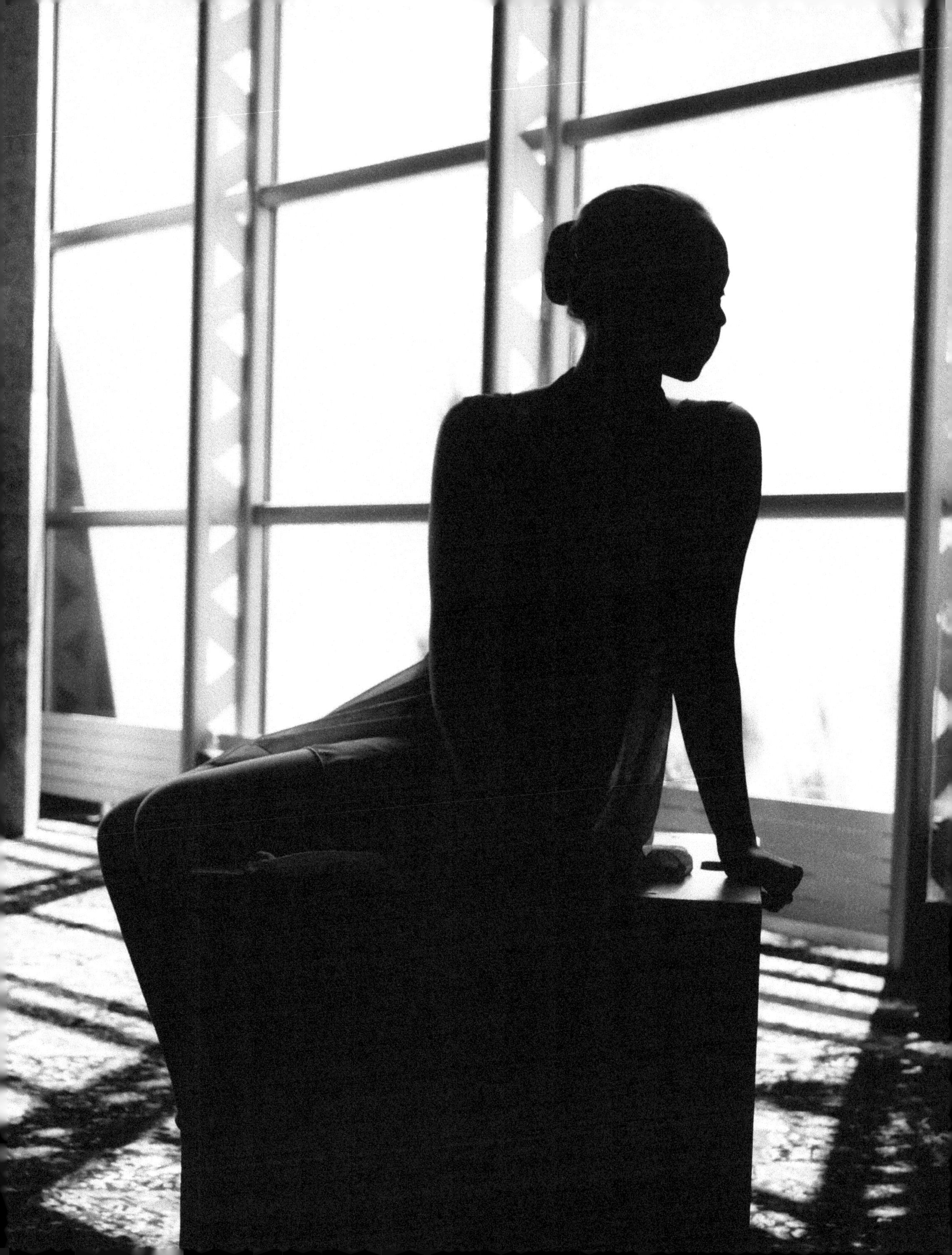

A little stage fright is good,
it gives you an edge

Make an entrance

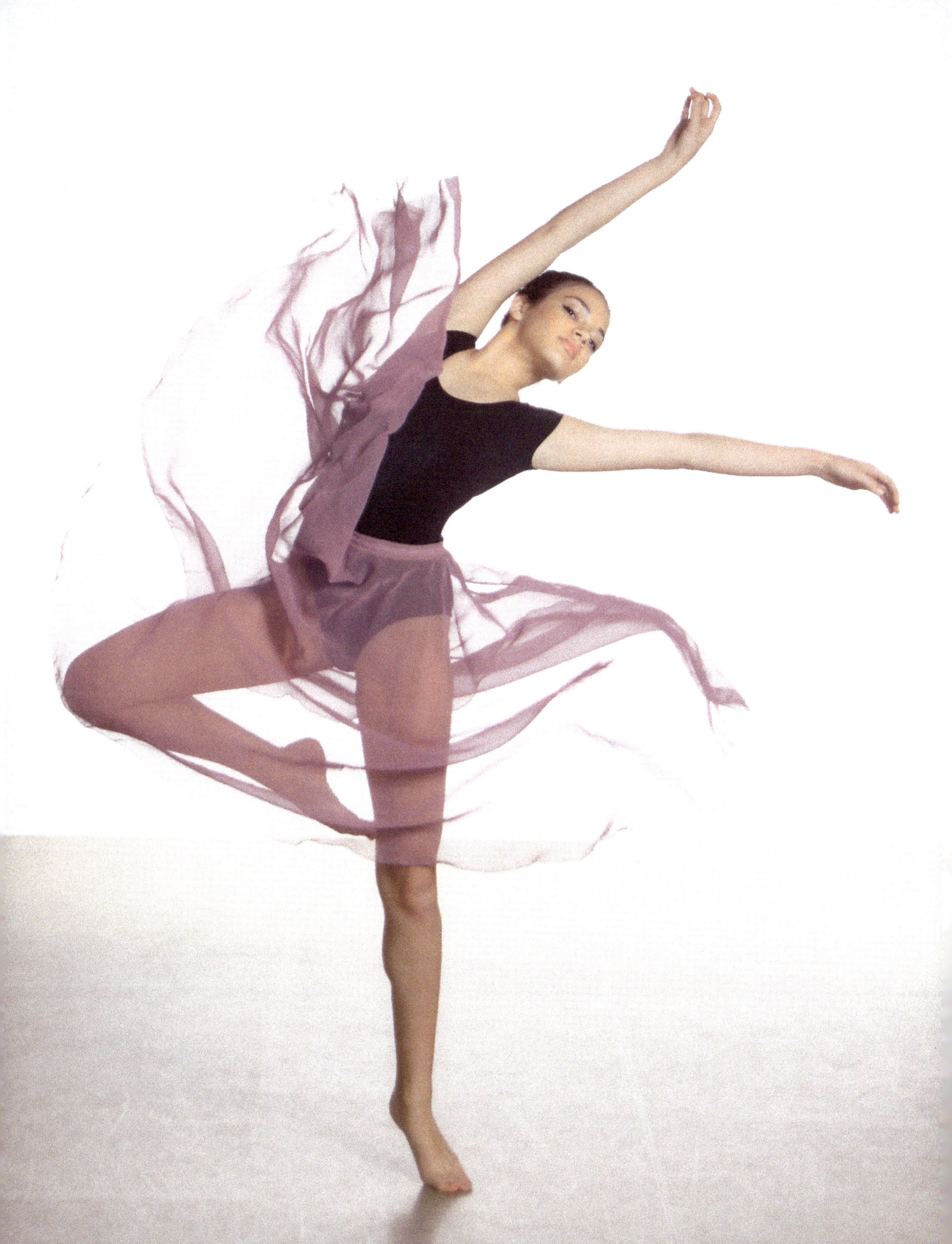

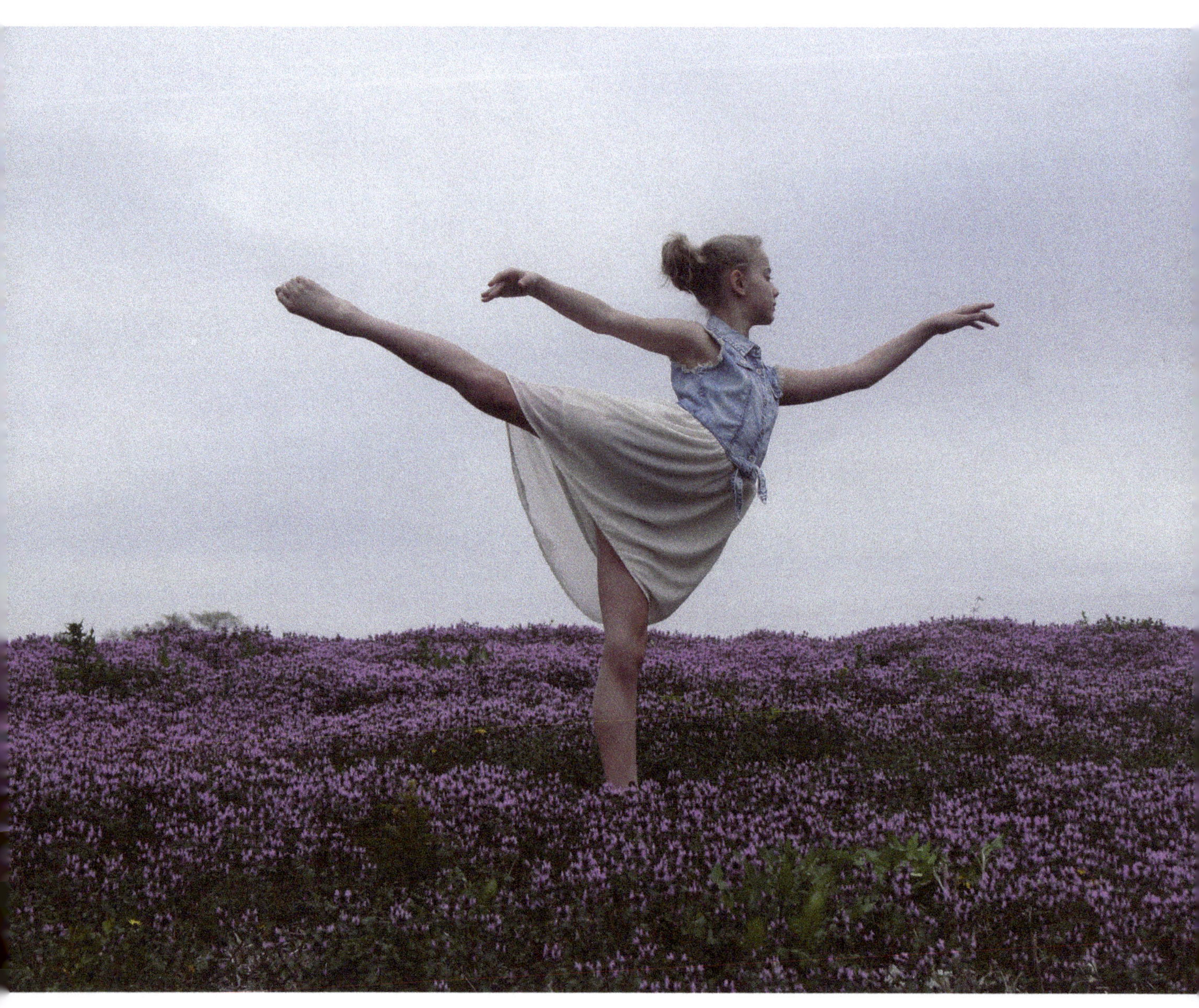

Look up and out,
for that is where you will land

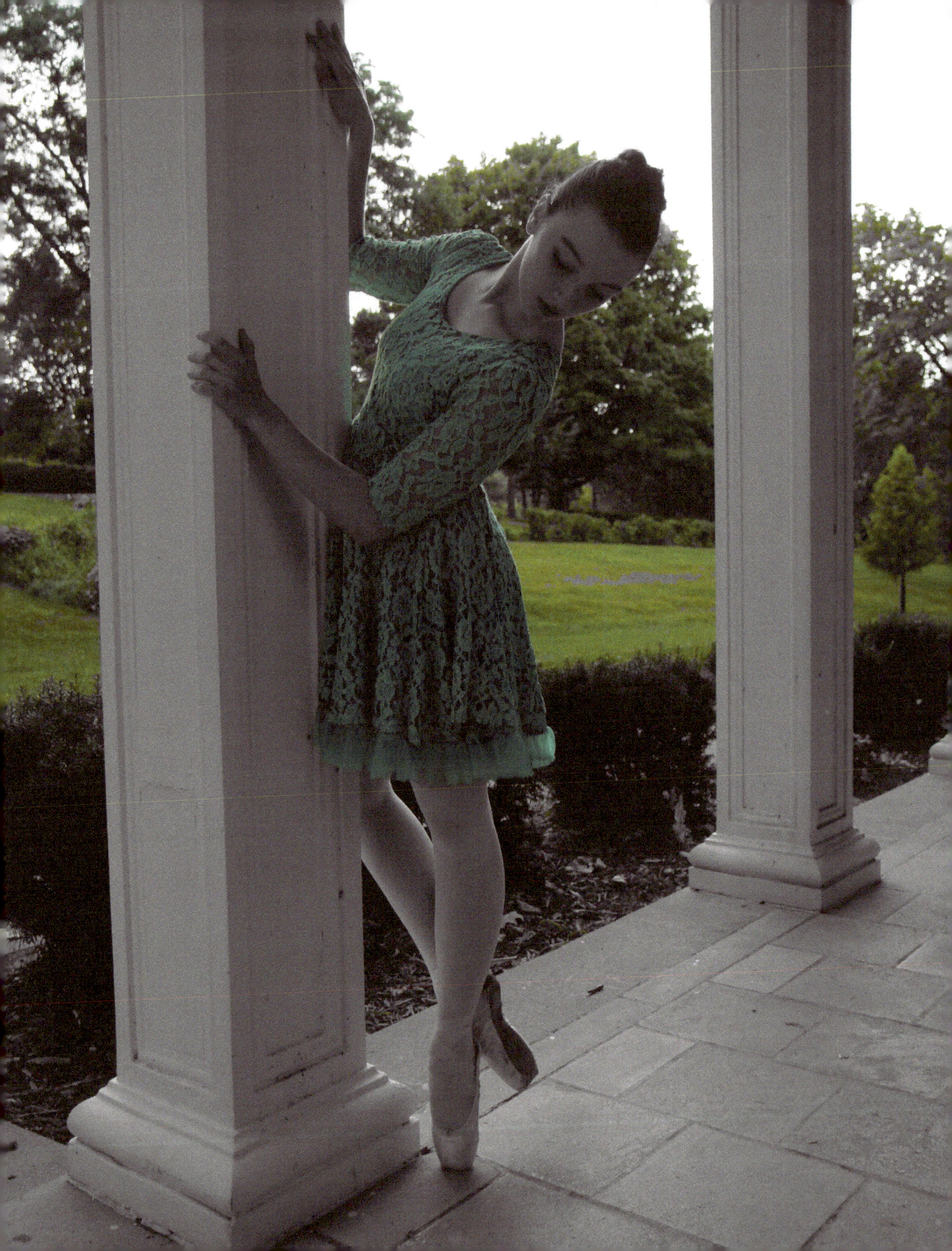

Fill the space you are given

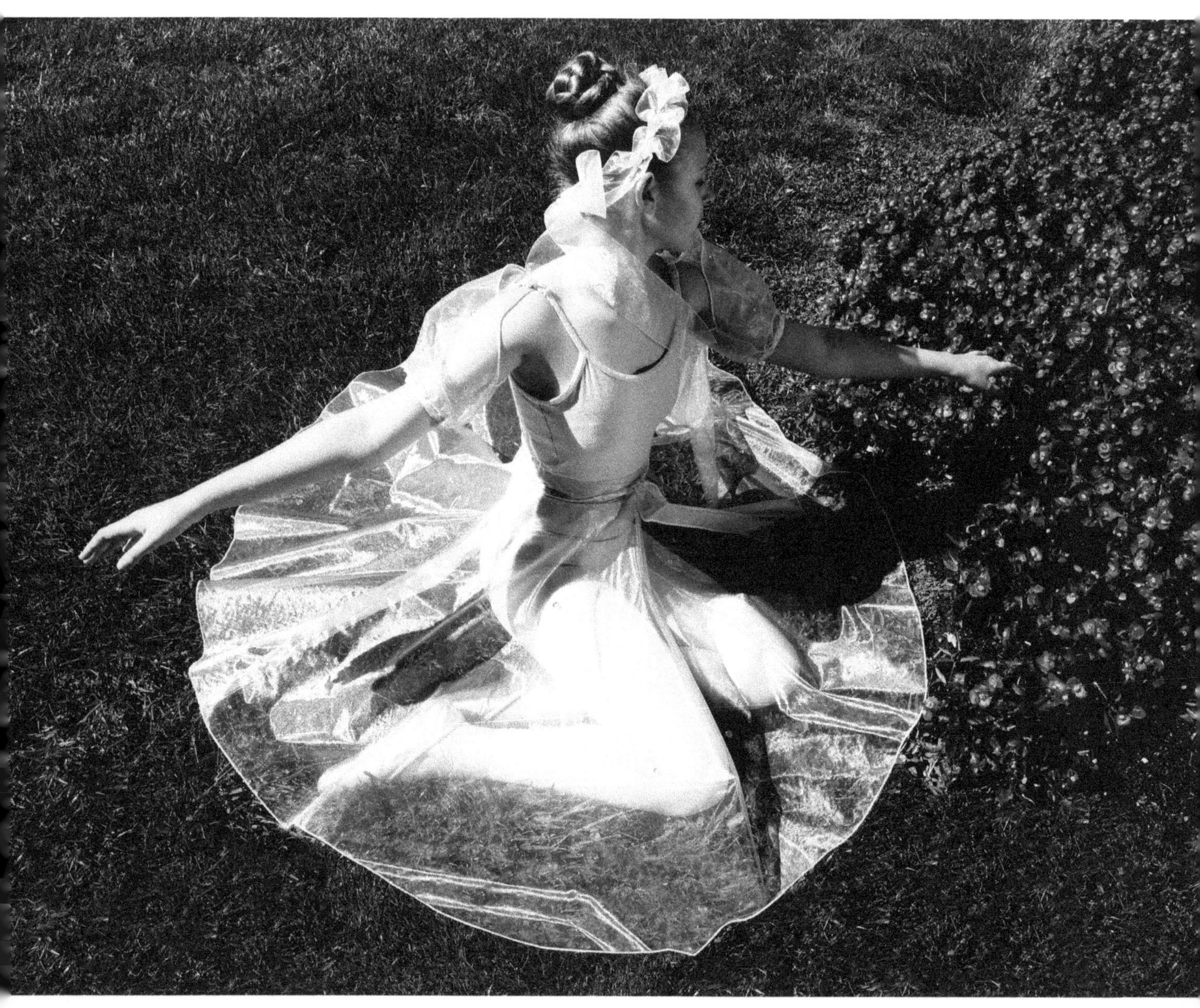

Be intentional

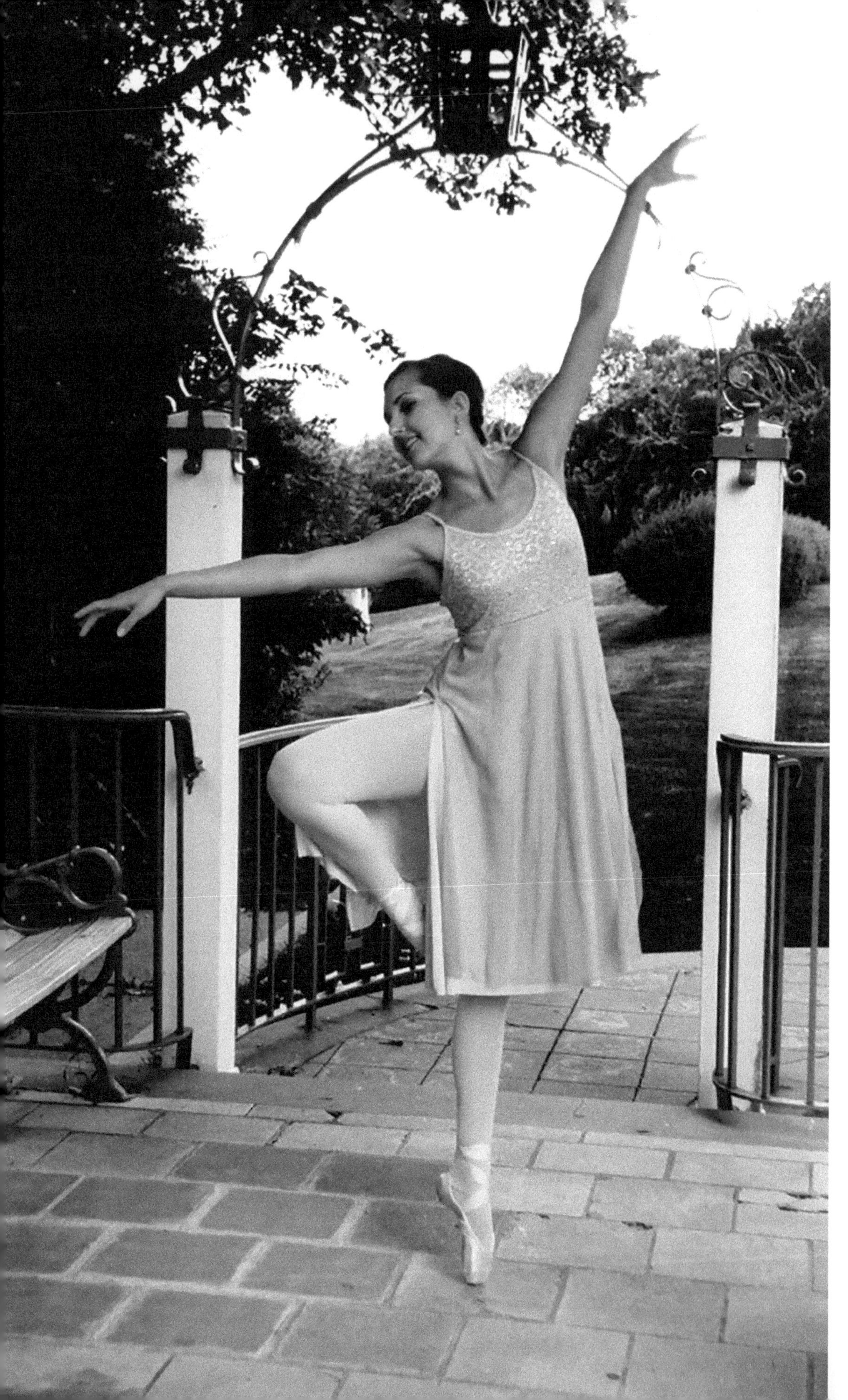

Live in the moment

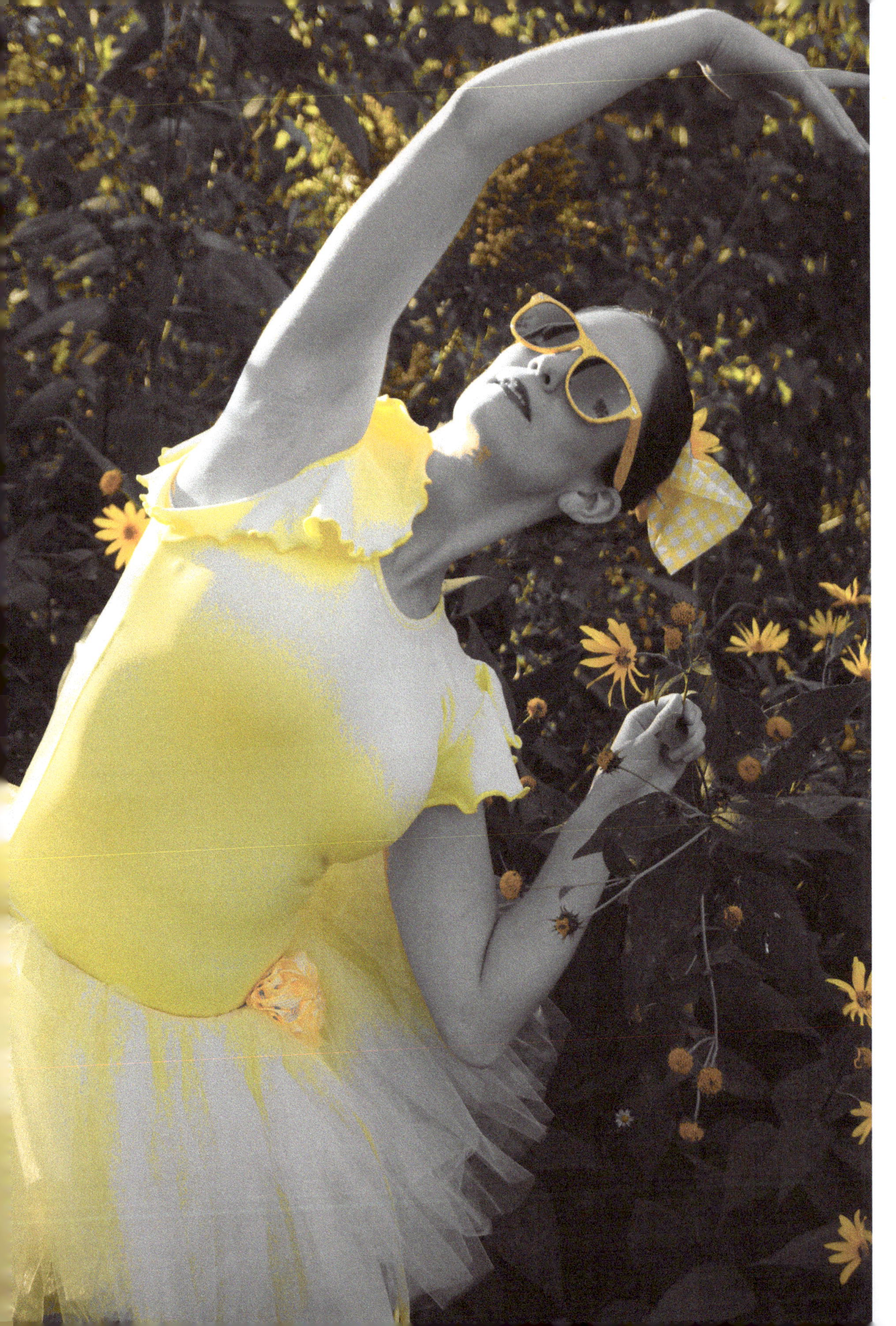

Think,
Process…
Do something

Begin again...
and again...
and again

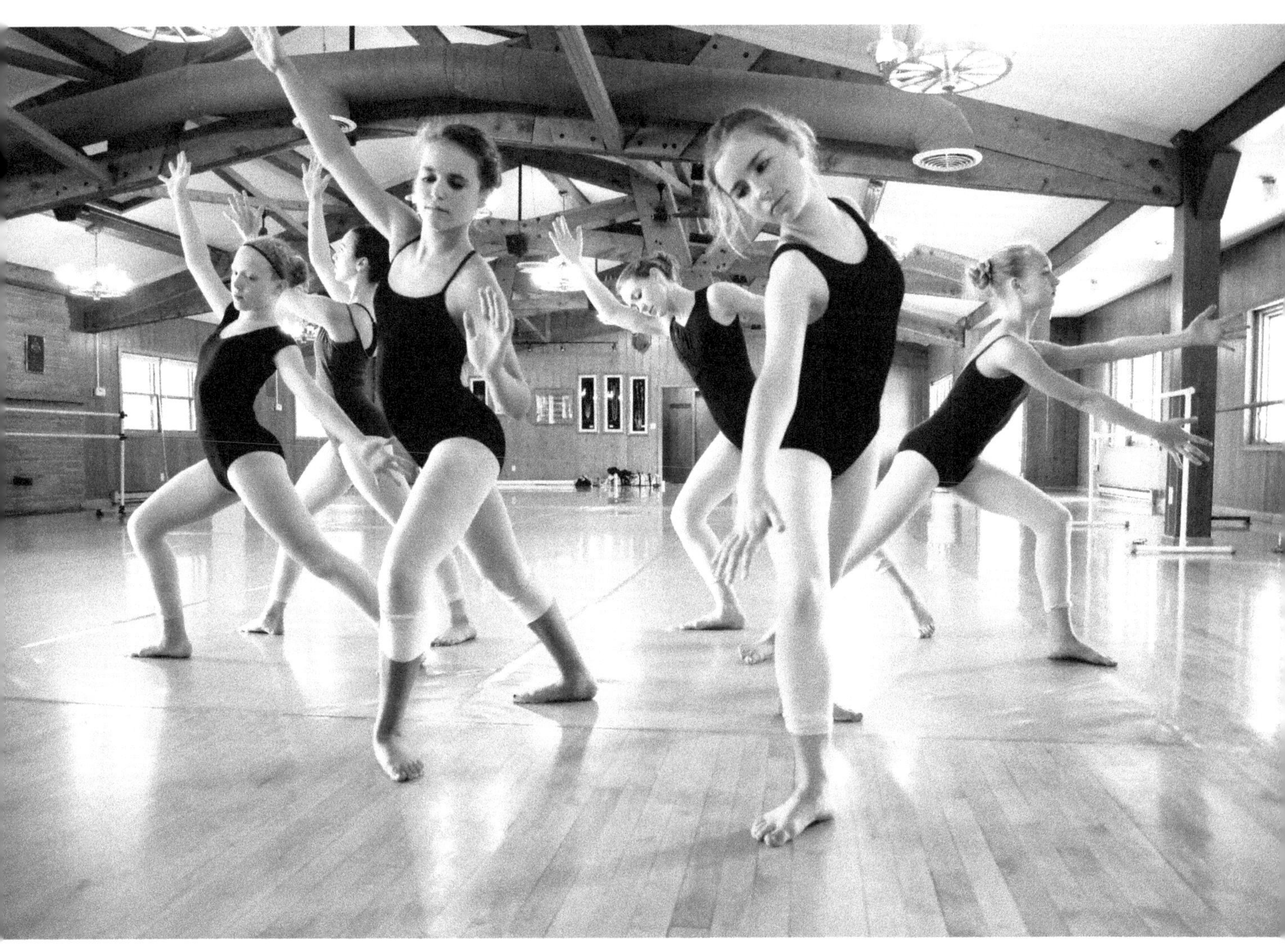

Technique is mastering the rules…
Learn when and how to break them

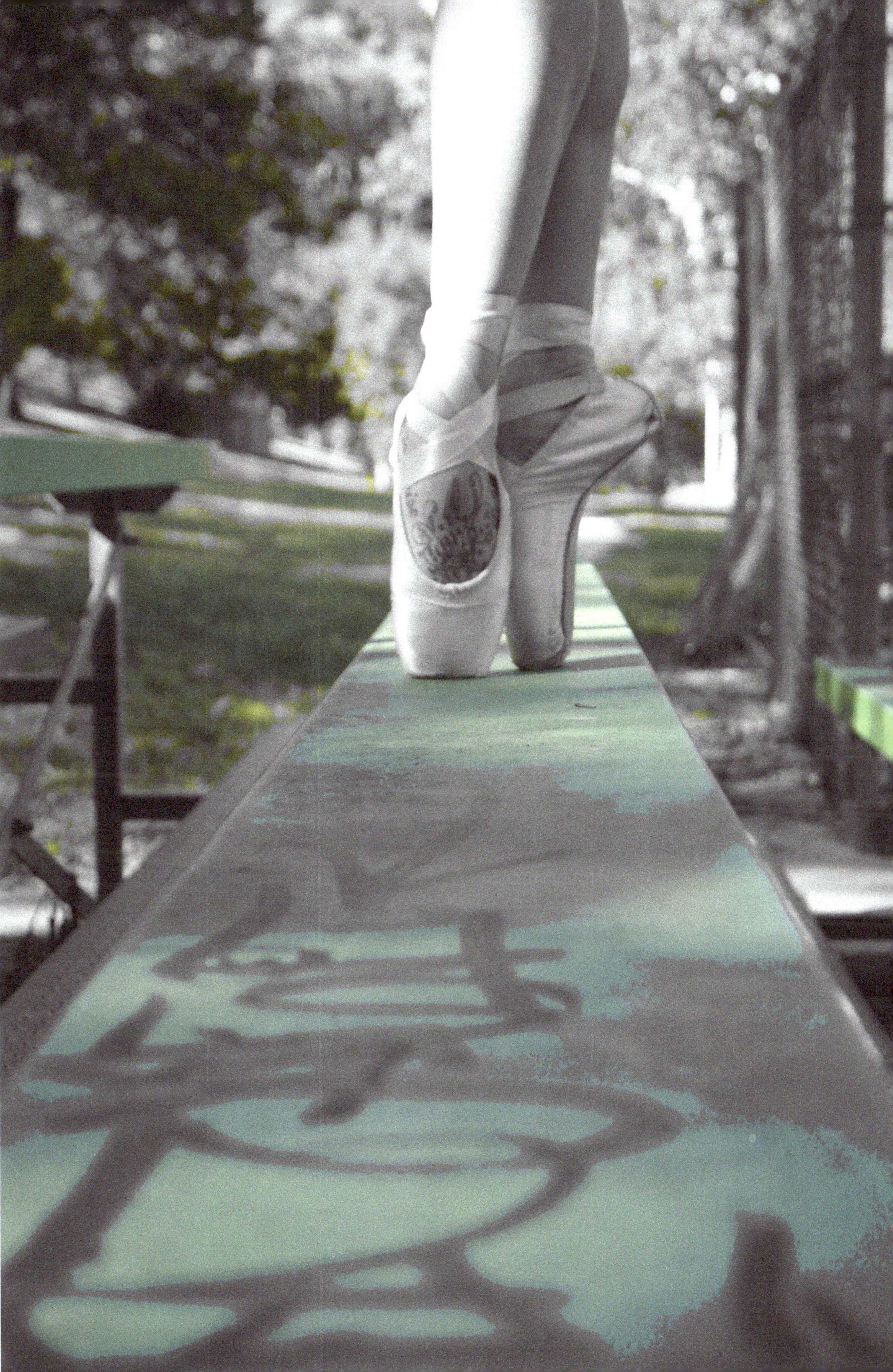

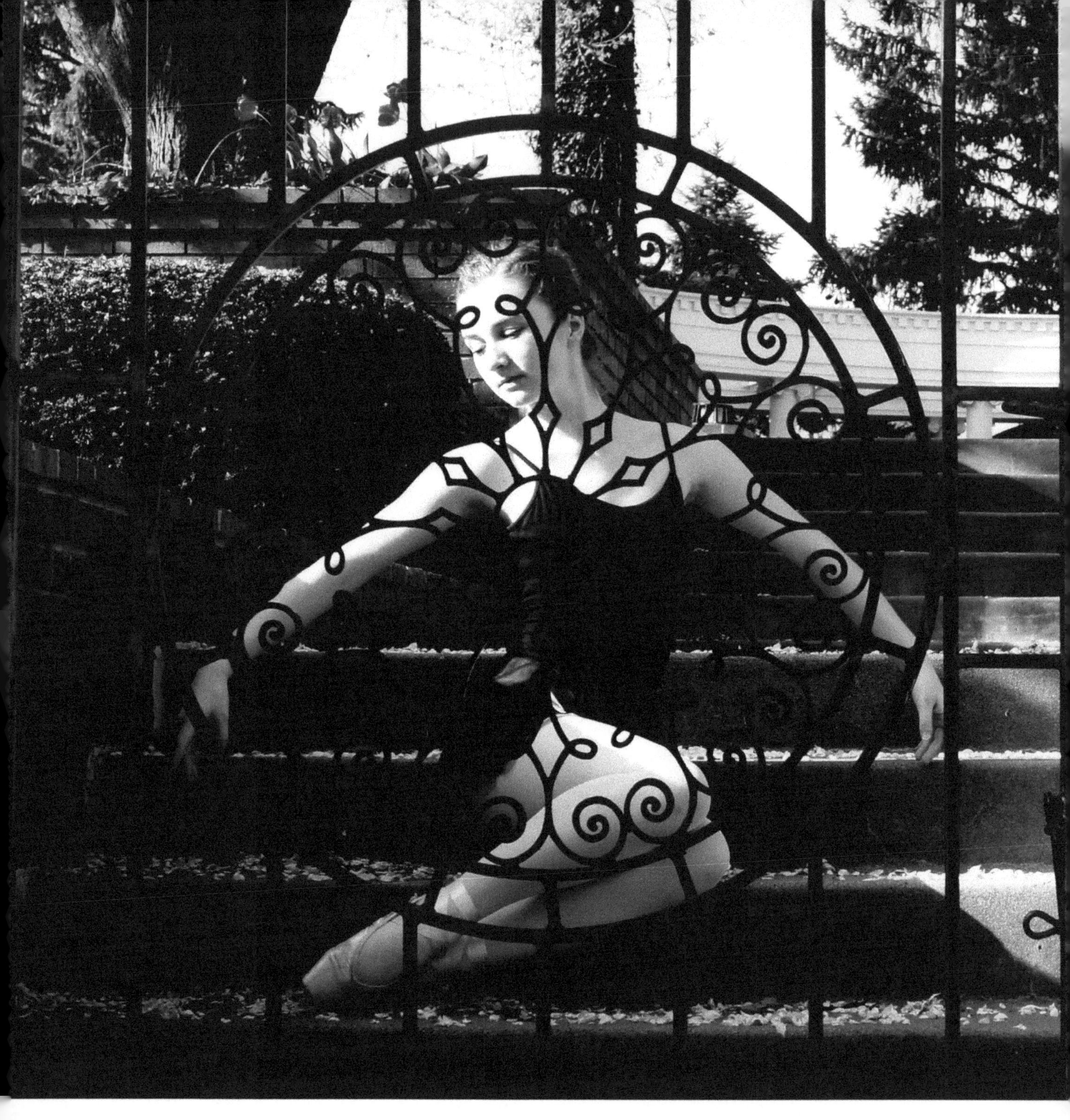

Accept compliments graciously,
accept criticism graciously

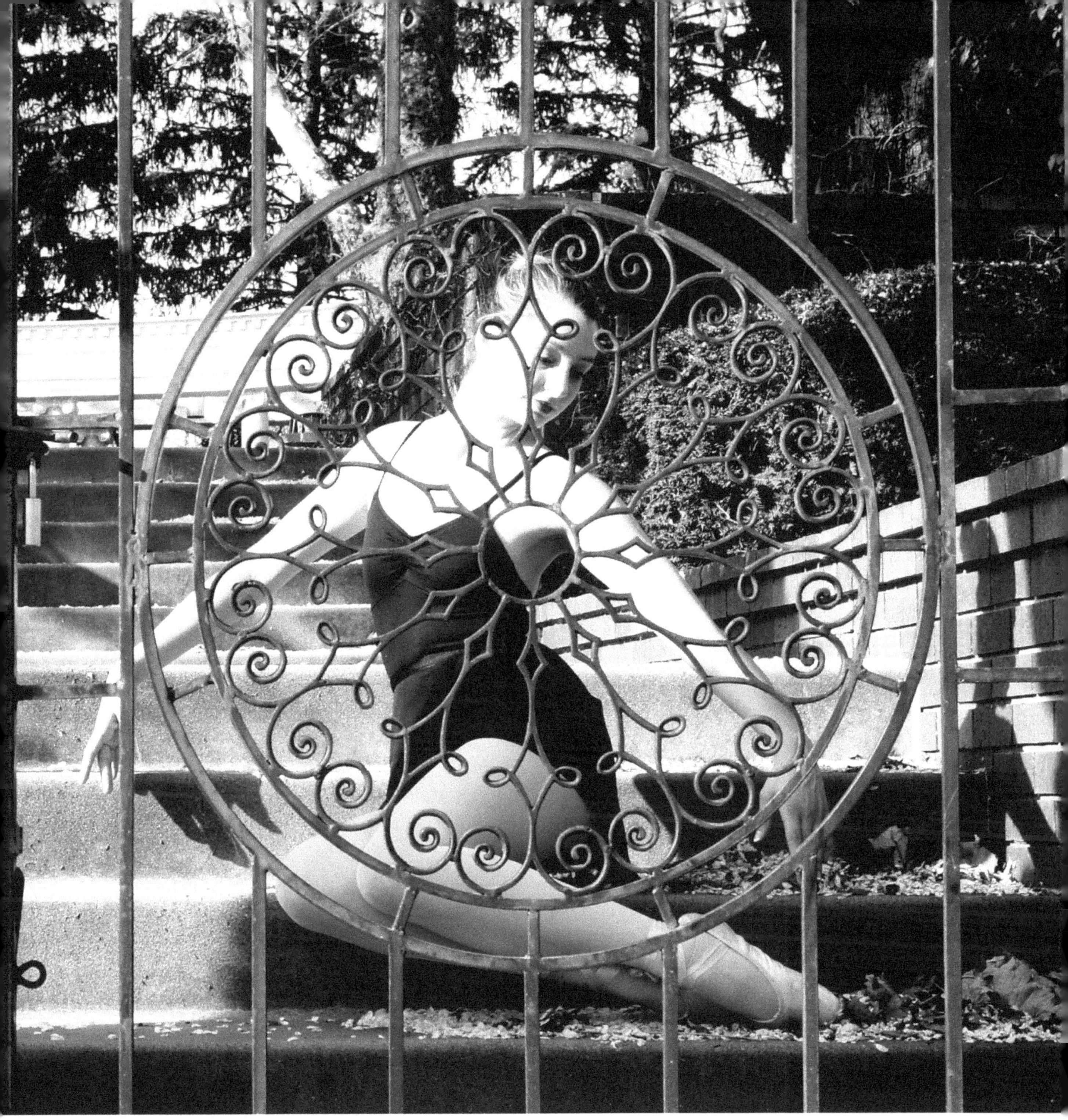

Take the good,
and learn from the bad

Remember…
movement doesn't lie

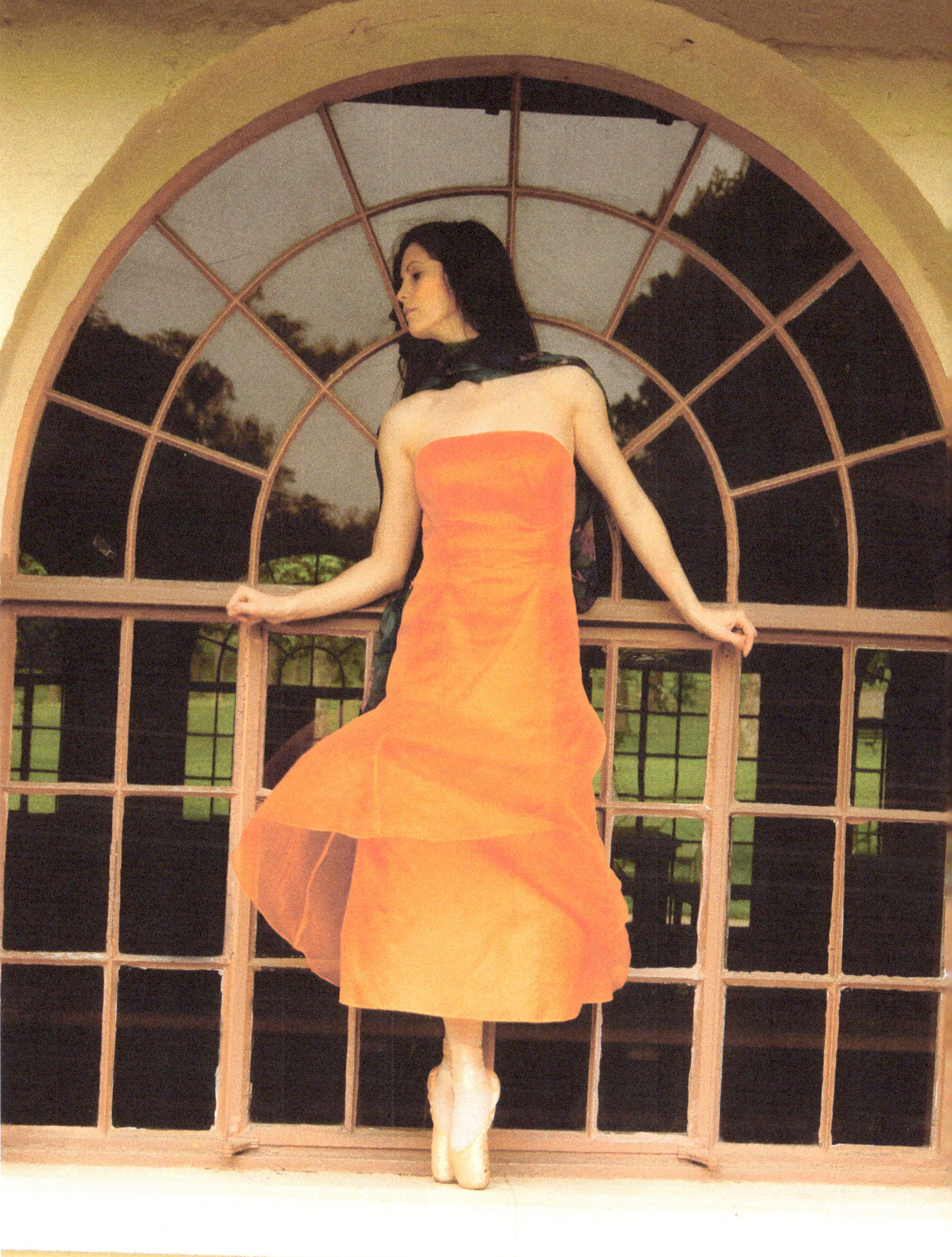

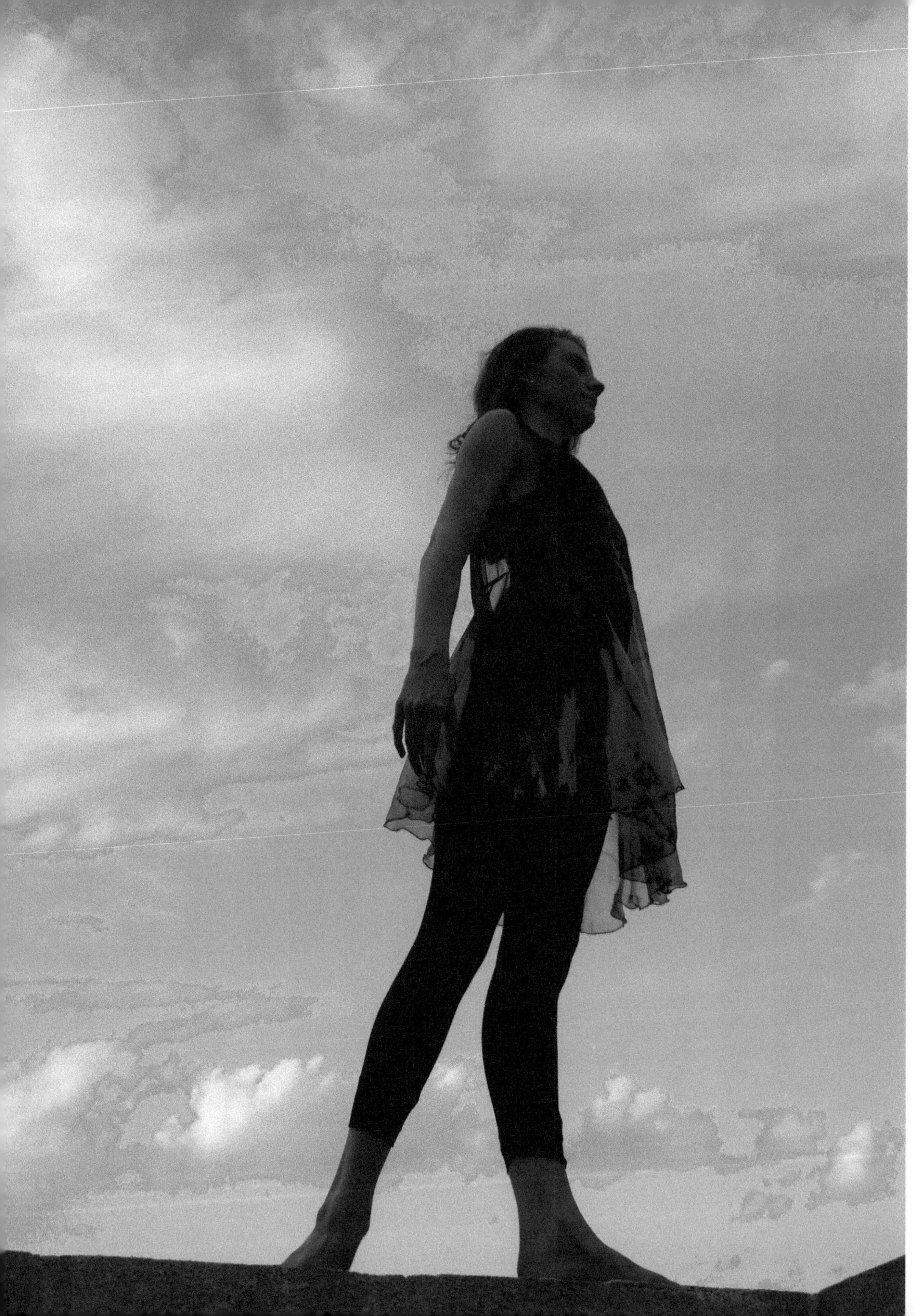

Listen

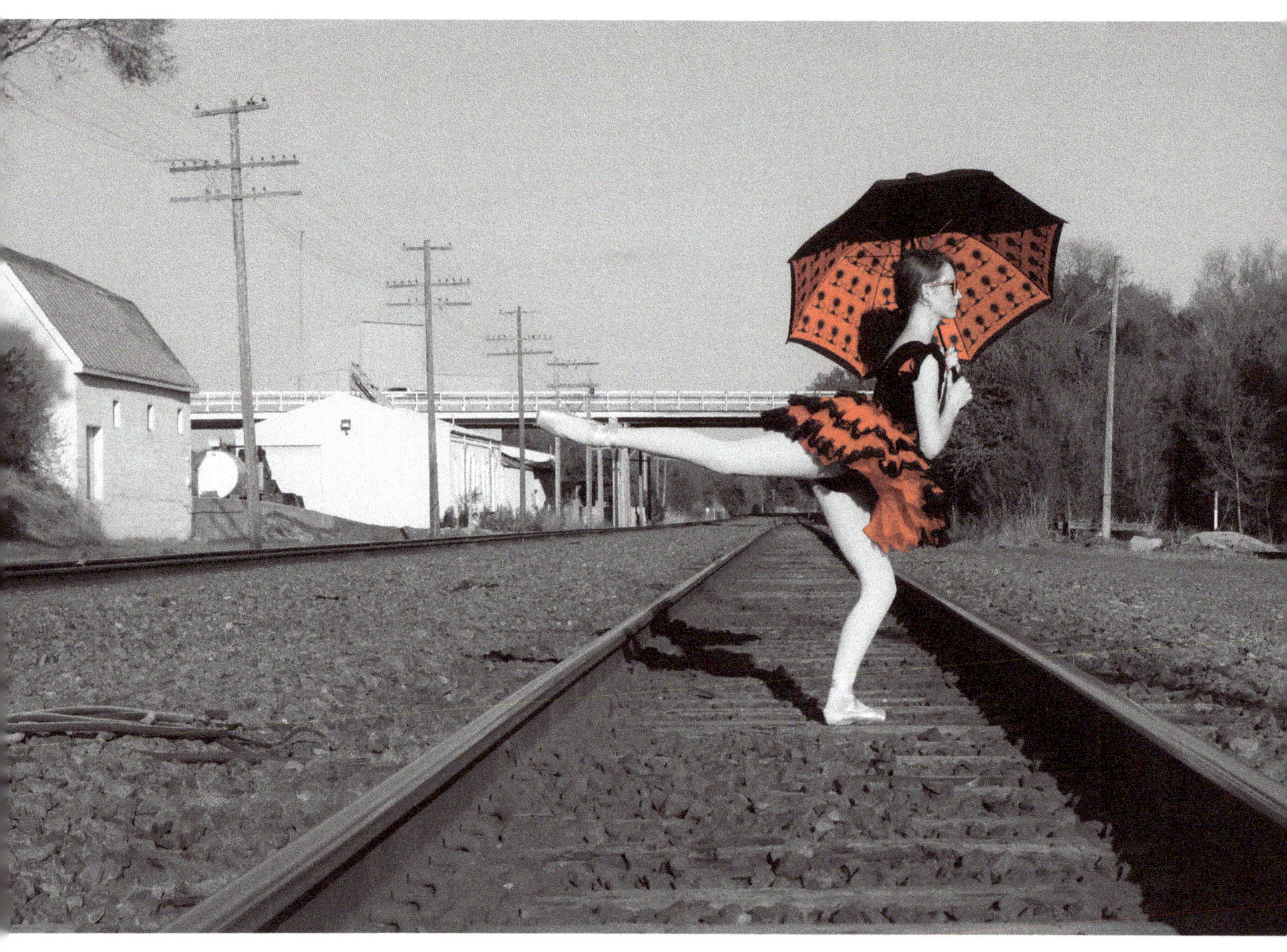

Take a risk

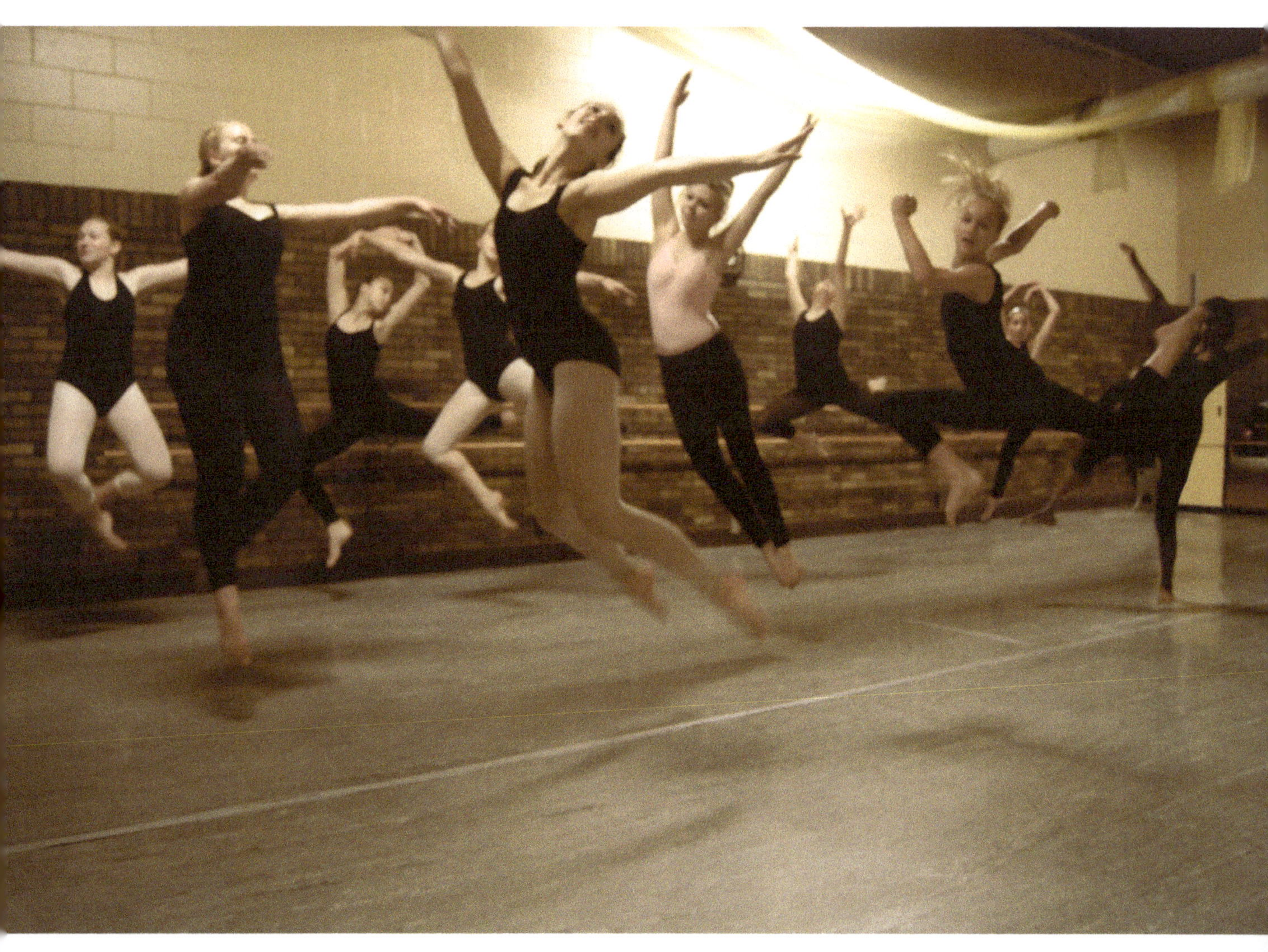

Be open to possibilities

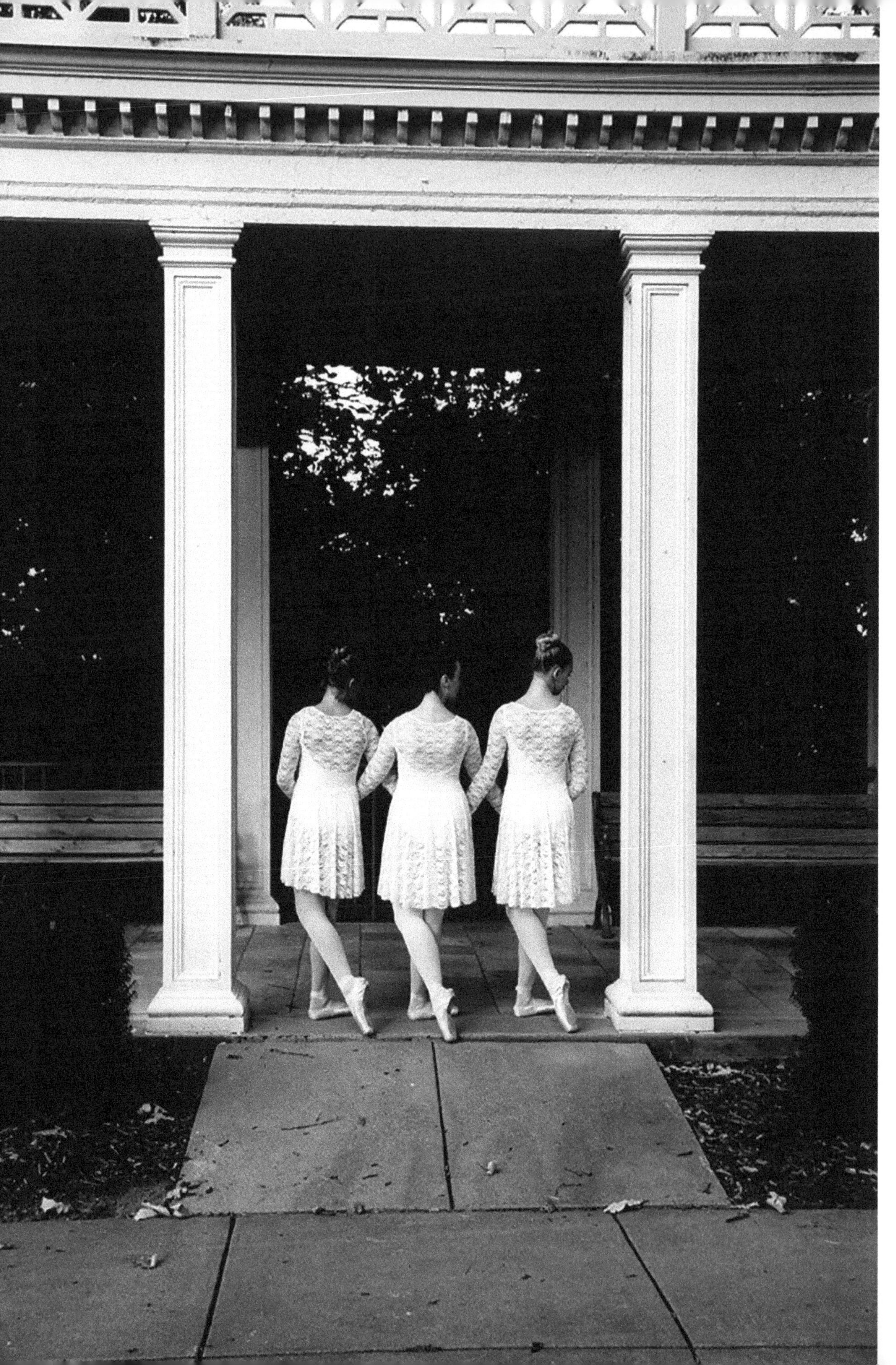

Strive for excellence,
and perfection will come

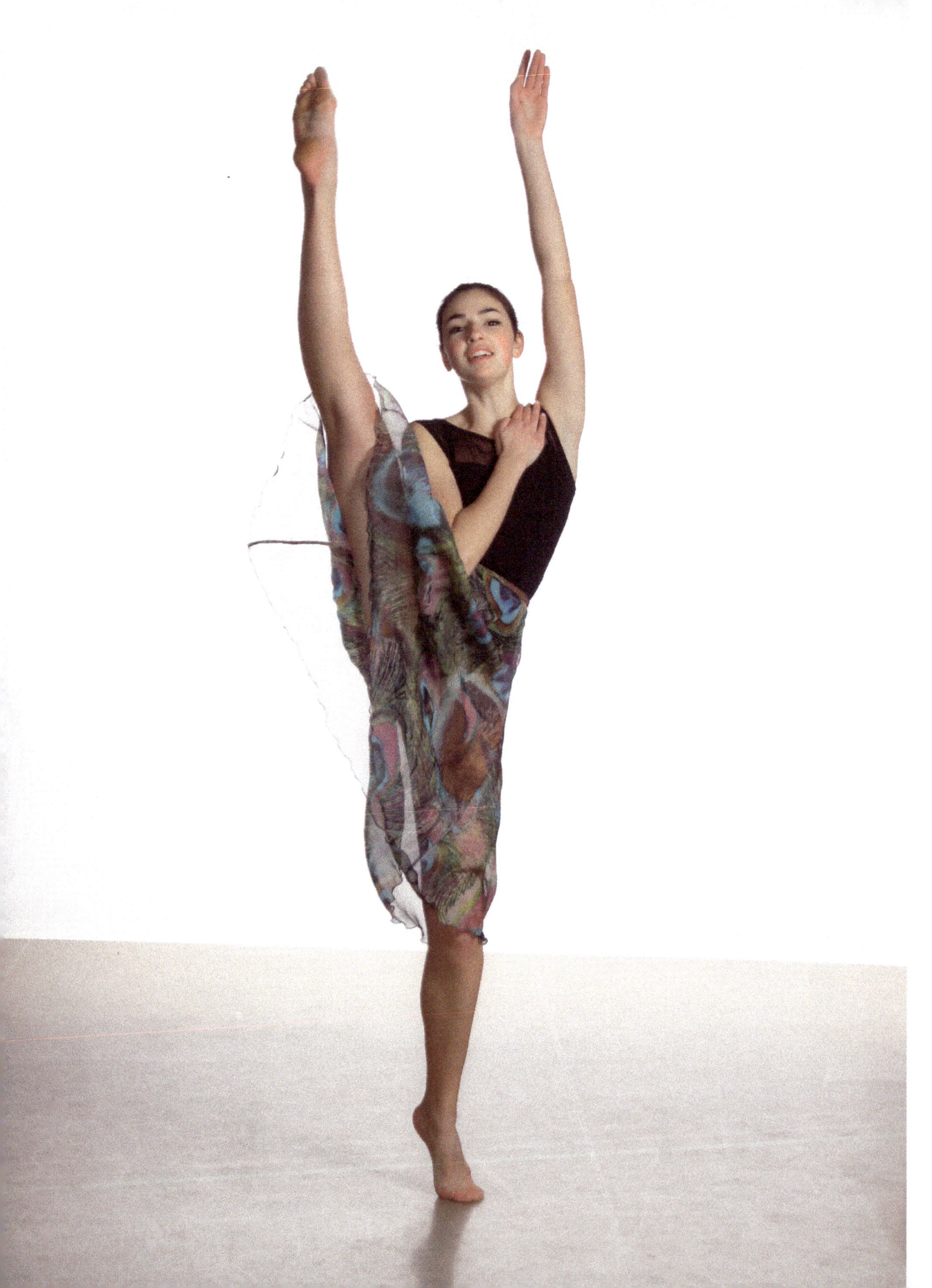

Make a big finish,
End on a high note

Thank your audience

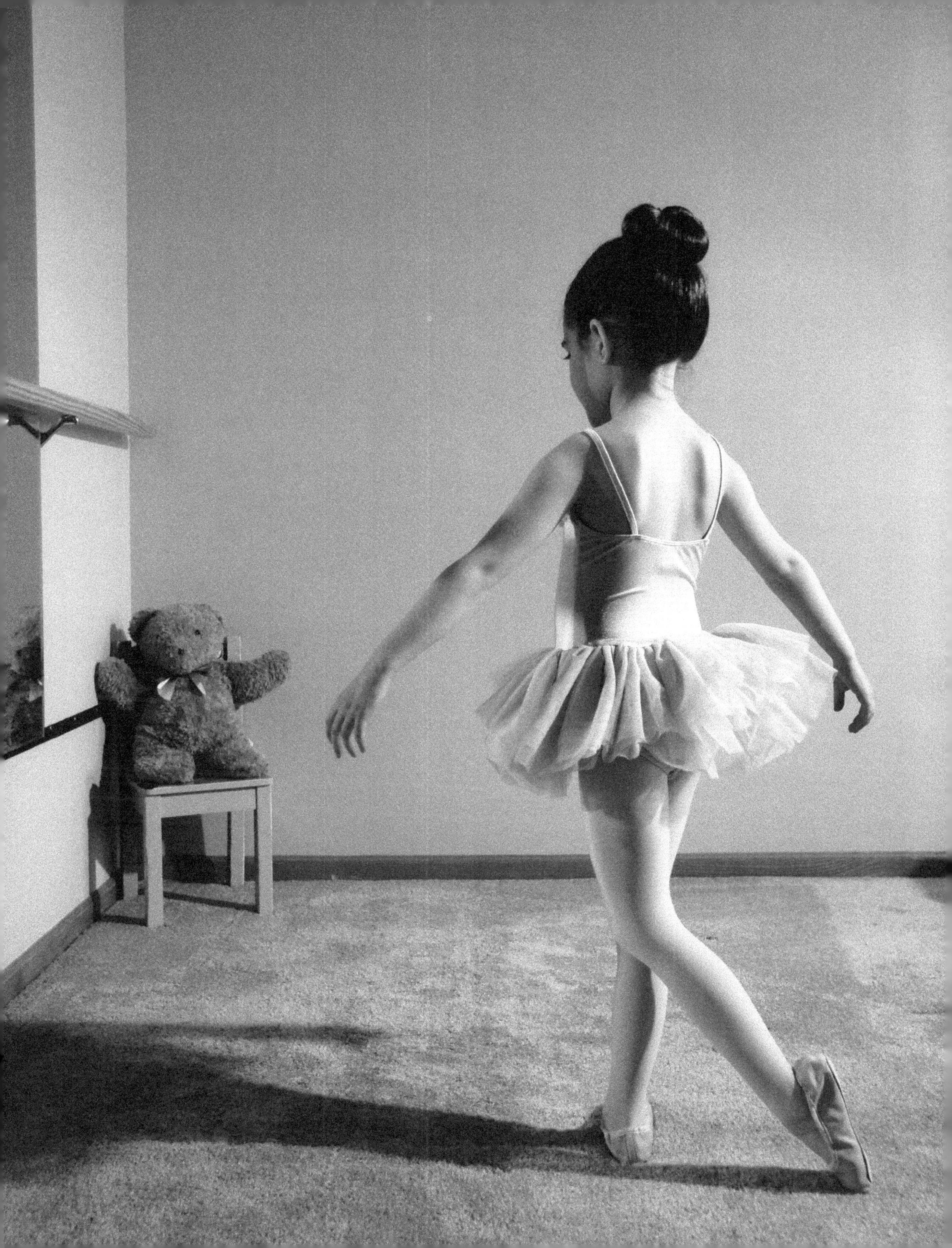

About the Author

Julian Adair is a noted choreographer, dance educator, performer, writer, arts photographer and director. She began her formal dance training in 1973 and earned a B.F.A. in dance from Creighton University in 1987. Having performed and choreographed professionally throughout the Midwest, there are more than 130 productions to her credit. She is a two-time recipient of the Theater Arts Guild Outstanding Achievement in Choreography Award and winner of the Omaha Entertainment and Arts Outstanding Choreographer. In 1993, Adair Dance Academy was founded, followed by Ever After Productions in 2006, both under Julian's direction, furthering her mission of promoting creativity and the performing arts through training, production opportunities and creative outlets.

As a child, Julian was able to see movement, color and texture in music and transferred these skills to the written page and photography. A regular contributor to literary journals, she has also exhibited her photographic work in Omaha and Los Angeles. Her photography records moments of choreography beyond the stage, using natural light, architecture and natural surroundings.

Julian is happily married to Steve Adair, and together they have two daughters, Camille and Colette, both accomplished performers.

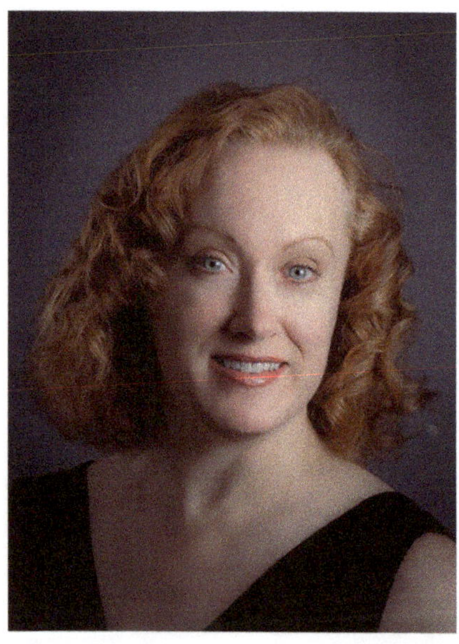